ARKANSAS PETITIONS 1800 [1795-1804] and
(Beginning Page 4)

ORLEANS TERRITORY (NOW LOUISIANA) PETITIONS, ETC., 1800 [1795-1804]
(Beginning Page 6)

United States, Department of State, compiled and edited by Clarence Edwin Carter, *The Territorial Papers of the United States* Washington, D.C.: Government Printing Office, 1934-1962. 26 volumes. National Archives microfilm publications: M0721
> vol. 1. The Territorial Papers of the United States, General.
> vols. II & III The Territory Northwest of the River Ohio, 1787-1803.
> vol. IV The Territory South of the River Ohio, 1790-1796.
> vols. V & VI The Territory of Mississippi, 1798-1817.
> vols. VII & VIII The Territory of Indiana, 1800-1816.
> vol. IX The Territory of Orleans, 1803-1812.
> vols. X - XII The Territory of Michigan, 1805-1837.
> vols. XIII - XV The Territory of Louisiana-Missouri, 1803-1821.
> vols. XVI & XVII The Territory of Illinois, 1809-1818.
> vol. XVIII The Territory of Alabama, 1817-1819.
> vols. XIX - XXI The Territory of Arkansas, 1819-1836.
> vols. XXII - XXVI The Territory of Florida, 1821-1845.

[Please note: *Larger lists of names, such as petitions, etc., will be entered into the database. Names found in regular governmental/public transactions that contain no individual biographical details will not be extracted.*]

LA-01 ARKANSAS PETITIONS 1800 [1795-1804] and ORLEANS TERRITORY (NOW LOUISIANA) PETITIONS, ETC., 1800 [1795-1804]. This book was compiled from *Territorial Papers of the United States* and contains 495 names for Louisiana and 3 from Arkansas. Since no federal census exists for Arkansas and Louisiana for 1800, these records nicely substitute for those missing documents. These records include an incredible amount of information about these early people. While the federal censuses are missing that would help track these people, these records are even better in some respects than the census because it helps us understand some of the challenges they faced. That is why this new book can help. Some additional biographical details may be included, plus possible relationships with other family members. For information on how to obtain this book search by the title or "Books by John Stemmons" at Amazon.com. This comes automatically with a paperback binding. It includes but is not limited to petitions regarding:
- Inhabitants of Pointe Coupee to Gov. Claiborne, requesting military aid because of fears of a slave revolt.
- Characterization of New Orleans residents, 1 July 1804.
- Address from the free people of color Jan. 1804, volunteering for military service.
- Memorial to Congress from merchants of New Orleans, 9 Jan 1804, offering allegiance to the US.
- Appointments about military and local officers, etc.

INDEXES

Indexes are expensive to compile.
Which is why many books do not have them. Most that do just have a simple name index. A noteworthy exception is the *Territorial Papers of the United States* which gives some limited context as explained below.
Indexes are expensive but using modern technology we at Stemmons Publishing have included nearly all the context you may need. 100% context is probably not possible such as in a census that lists multiple neighbors. Search for entries of the same page in our book(s) or the original document if you require more information.

PUBLICATIONS FROM STEMMONS PUBLISHING

These following publications are not just traditional alphabetical lists of names, they include the context of information with each name!!

Why is that so important? Because many of the names in our books were obtained from various sources including South Carolina jury lists, the *Territorial Papers of the United States* (28 volumes each with its own index), petitions, tax lists, etc., and like most books with indexes common names require a lot of time to check each entry in the index. Can you imagine how many Smiths you would have to go through page-by-page for a compilation the size of *Territorial Papers of the United States*? Their indexes provide some context such as signing a petition. No explanation is given of what, when, or why the petition was made. Because we have included the context with each name, you can easily search all the Smiths, Taylors, Browns, Williams, etc., without all the drudgery! And since most of us have common surnames, we may need some help. Now, the originals of the South Carolina jury lists are housed in the South Carolina Department of Archives and History. Therefore, you may not have access to the originals. The way we index names means it is almost as good as being at the Archives yourself and doubly so since these documents are loose papers and do not have an original index. Our books provide an enhanced way of using *Territorial Papers of the United States* that the original compilers did not envision. So, if you have this collection, your obtaining our books compiled from those volumes will help your access to *Territorial Papers of the United States* even if you are not interested in our books about South Carolina jury lists. Now, that's what I call achieving the potential of a real index! It takes the bare skeleton of a name on a list and covers it with the flesh, hair, eyes, etc., of a human body. The names are more able to stand alone by themselves than is the case with a traditional index. We did not index subjects. *Territorial Papers of the United States* did.

Checking a name from our books and going to the page in *Territorial Papers of the United States* will show the list of names. Those listed next to the person of interest may be neighbors and relatives.

3

3 Names

Winters, Elisha,   Louisiana   Arkansas District
          Winters, Elisha,   Male
Protest, 4 Oct 1819, to the President from Joshua G. Clarke of Claiborne County, Mississippi against lands granted to Elisha Winters, William Winters, and Gabl Winters by the King of Spain being surveyed for Military Bounty land [pp. 114-5].
"Joshua G. Clarke to the President
STATE OF MISSISSIPPI, CLAIBORNE COUNTY, G PORT, 4 Octo 1819
To his Excellency, the President of the U States.
A Protest.

BE IT KNOWN, That the Governor Genl of the late Province of Louisiana, when under the Dominion of the King of Spain. On the twenty seventh day of June, in the year of our lord, one thousand, seven hundred & ninety seven; did Grant, to Elisha Winters, one Million Arpents of Land, to William Winters & Gabl Winters, sons of Elisha Winters, each, two Hundred & fifty thousands Arpents, of Land; to be located, in the District of Arkansas, by the Commandant who was charged, with the location of said Concessions— And be it further Known, that Elisha Winters & William Winters, were put into the Possession of the lands, so granted; and the boundary & courses designated, & Seisin given by the Commandant, in due form; in the Spring of 1798. That Gabl Winter, being a Minor, his lands were designated.

And be it, further Known, that all the Conditions, of the Grants to Elisha Winters & William Winters, were complied with, & that the said Elisha & William Winters, by themselves & tenants & grantees have been in the actual & quiet & peaceable possessions of said lands since the Spring of the year, One thousand seven hundred & ninety eight, & which lands are now in the quiet & peaceable possession of the said Heirs & grantees of the said Elisha & William Winters. And be

[page 115] it further Known, that legal Entries, of said Lands, were made, in the Land office of the U States, at St Louis & the Title papers & other evidence, were filed, according to the provisions of the several acts of Congress, for the final adjustment of the land Titles of said Territory.

And be it further known, that said claims are now pending before the Congress of the U. States. That the H of Representatives of the U S. at their Session of 1817, did by a Select Committee, Report in favor of Confirming the titles, of Elisha & William Winters; which Report is still pending & undecided by the Congress of the U S.

And whereas it appears, that the Surveyors, under the authority of the U States, are now locating & laying off, said Lands, for Military bounty lands; thereby interfering with the rights & interests of the Undersigned, & his Co-tenants in Common.—

The undersigned, for himself & his Co-tenants in Common, in the said grants of Lands, to Elisha Winters William Winters & Gabl Winters, Solomnly protests, against the surveying or disposing of said lands, or any part thereof, by the United States, as Military bounty lands, or otherwise; until the titles of the Claimants of said lands, are decided by Congress, or some Competent tribunal according to Law.

And the Undersigned, further respectfully desires, that this Protest, may be entd as a Caveat, in the Proper Office, agt the issuing any Patent, from the U. States, for said lands; until their rights are adjudicated & determined by a Competent Tribunal.

Which Protest, is respectfully, Submitted, to the Consideration of the President of the U States by
                              J   G CLARKE
                              for himself & Co-tenants in Common." [pp. 114-5]

Territorial Papers of the US - volume: 19 page: 114

Winters, Gabl, Louisiana Arkansas District

Winters, Gabl, Male
Protest, 4 Oct 1819, to the President from Joshua G. Clarke of Claiborne County, Mississippi against lands granted to Elisha Winters, William Winters, and Gabl Winters by the King of Spain being surveyed for Military Bounty land [pp. 114-5].
"Joshua G. Clarke to the President
STATE OF MISSISSIPPI, CLAIBORNE COUNTY, G PORT, 4 Octo 1819
To his Excellency, the President of the U States.
A Protest.

BE IT KNOWN, That the Governor Genl of the late Province of Louisiana, when under the Dominion of the King of Spain. On the twenty seventh day of June, in the year of our lord, one thousand, seven hundred & ninety seven; did Grant, to Elisha Winters, one Million Arpents of Land, to William Winters & Gabl Winters, sons of Elisha Winters, each, two Hundred & fifty thousands Arpents, of Land; to be located, in the District of Arkansas, by the Commandant who was charged, with the location of said Concessions— And be it further Known, that Elisha Winters & William Winters, were put into the Possession of the lands, so granted; and the boundary & courses designated, & Seisin given by the Commandant, in due form; in the Spring of 1798. That Gabl Winter, being a Minor, his lands were designated.

And be it, further Known, that all the Conditions, of the Grants to Elisha Winters & William Winters, were complied with, & that the said Elisha & William Winters, by themselves & tenants & grantees have been in the actual & quiet & peaceable possessions of said lands since the Spring of the year, One thousand seven hundred & ninety eight, & which lands are now in the quiet & peaceable possession of the said Heirs & grantees of the said Elisha & William Winters. And be [page 115] it further Known, that legal Entries, of said Lands, were made, in the Land office of the U States, at St Louis & the Title papers & other evidence, were filed, according to the provisions of the several acts of Congress, for the final adjustment of the land Titles of said Territory.

And be it further known, that said claims are now pending before the Congress of the U. States.

That the H of Representatives of the U S. at their Session of 1817, did by a Select Committee, Report in favor of Confirming the titles, of Elisha & William Winters; which Report is still pending & undecided by the Congress of the U S.

And whereas it appears, that the Surveyors, under the authority of the U States, are now locating & laying off, said Lands, for Military bounty lands; thereby interfering with the rights & interests of the Undersigned, & his Co-tenants in Common.—

The undersigned, for himself & his Co-tenants in Common, in the said grants of Lands, to Elisha Winters William Winters & Gabl Winters, Solomnly protests, against the surveying or disposing of said lands, or any part thereof, by the United States, as Military bounty lands, or otherwise; until the titles of the Claimants of said lands, are decided by Congress, or some Competent tribunal according to Law.

And the Undersigned, further respectfully desires, that this Protest, may be entd as a Caveat, in the Proper Office, agt the issuing any Patent, from the U. States, for said lands; until their rights are adjudicated & determined by a Competent Tribunal.

Which Protest, is respectfully, Submitted, to the Consideration of the President of the U States by

J G CLARKE

for himself & Co-tenants in Common." [pp. 114-5]
Territorial Papers of the US - volume: 19 page: 114

Winters, William, Louisiana Arkansas District

Winters, William, Male
Protest, 4 Oct 1819, to the President from Joshua G. Clarke of Claiborne County, Mississippi against lands granted to Elisha Winters, William Winters, and Gabl Winters by the King of Spain being surveyed for Military Bounty land [pp. 114-5].
"Joshua G. Clarke to the President
STATE OF MISSISSIPPI, CLAIBORNE COUNTY, G PORT, 4 Octo 1819
To his Excellency, the President of the U States.
A Protest.

BE IT KNOWN, That the Governor Genl of the late Province of Louisiana, when under the Dominion of the King of Spain. On the twenty seventh day of June, in the year of our lord, one thousand, seven hundred & ninety seven; did Grant, to Elisha Winters, one Million Arpents of Land, to William Winters & Gabl Winters, sons of Elisha Winters, each, two Hundred & fifty thousands Arpents, of Land; to be located, in the District of Arkansas, by the Commandant who was charged, with the location of said Concessions— And be it further Known, that Elisha Winters & William Winters, were put into the Possession of the lands, so granted; and the boundary & courses designated, & Seisin given by the Commandant, in due form; in the Spring of 1798. That Gabl Winter, being a Minor, his lands were designated.

And be it, further Known, that all the Conditions, of the Grants to Elisha Winters & William Winters, were complied with, & that the said Elisha & William Winters, by themselves & tenants & grantees have been in the actual & quiet & peaceable possessions of said lands since the Spring of the year, One thousand seven hundred & ninety eight, & which lands are now in the quiet & peaceable possession of the said Heirs & grantees of the said Elisha & William Winters. And be [page 115] it further Known, that legal Entries, of said Lands, were made, in the Land office of the U States, at St Louis & the Title papers & other evidence, were filed, according to the provisions of the several acts of Congress, for the final adjustment of the land Titles of said Territory.

And be it further known, that said claims are now pending before the Congress of the U. States. That the H of Representatives of the U S. at their Session of 1817, did by a Select Committee, Report in favor of Confirming the titles, of Elisha & William Winters; which Report is still pending & undecided by the Congress of the U S.

And whereas it appears, that the Surveyors, under the authority of the U States, are now locating & laying off, said Lands, for Military bounty lands; thereby interfering with the rights & interests of the Undersigned, & his Co-tenants in Common.—

The undersigned, for himself & his Co-tenants in Common, in the said grants of Lands, to Elisha Winters William Winters & Gabl Winters, Solomnly protests, against the surveying or disposing of said lands, or any part thereof, by the United States, as Military bounty lands, or otherwise; until the titles of the Claimants of said lands, are decided by Congress, or some Competent tribunal according to Law.

And the Undersigned, further respectfully desires, that this Protest, may be entd as a Caveat, in the Proper Office, agt the issuing any Patent, from the U. States, for said lands; until their rights are adjudicated & determined by a Competent Tribunal.

Which Protest, is respectfully, Submitted, to the Consideration of the President of the U States by

J   G

CLARKE

for himself & Co-
tenants in Common." [pp. 114-5]
Territorial Papers of the US - volume: 19 page: 114

LOUISIANA 1800 [1795-1804]

495 Names

Fabre "neveu", Jacque,   Orleans Territory
    Fabre "neveu", Jacque, Male
Petition, 9 Nov 1804, by inhabitants of Pointe Coupee to Gov. Claiborne, requesting military aid because of fears of a slave revolt.
Territorial Papers of the US - volume: 9 page: 327
[MS. Illegible],   Orleans Territory, New Orleans

[MS. Illegible], Male
Petition, 17 Sep 1804, by inhabitants & colonists of LA to Gov. Claiborne, requesting a commission be established for fear of a slave revolt.
Territorial Papers of the US - volume: 9 page: 296
Adam, F,   Orleans Territory, New Orleans
    Adam, F,   Male

Petition, 17 Sep 1804, by inhabitants & colonists of LA to Gov. Claiborne, requesting a commission be established for fear of a slave revolt.
Territorial Papers of the US - volume: 9 page: 296
Aigles, Baptiste d,   Orleans Territory
Aigles, Baptiste d,   Male **Color:** Colored
Address from the free people of color Jan. 1804, volunteering for military service
Territorial Papers of the US - volume: 9 page: 175
Allain, Au,   Orleans Territory
Allain, Au,   Male
Petition, 9 Nov 1804, by inhabitants of Pointe Coupee to Gov. Claiborne, requesting military aid because of fears of a slave revolt.
Territorial Papers of the US - volume: 9 page: 327
Allain, Frs,   Orleans Territory
Allain, Frs,   Male
Petition, 9 Nov 1804, by inhabitants of Pointe Coupee to Gov. Claiborne, requesting military aid because of fears of a slave revolt.
Territorial Papers of the US - volume: 9 page: 327
Allain, Zenon, Orleans Territory
Allain, Zenon,   Male
Petition, 9 Nov 1804, by inhabitants of Pointe Coupee to Gov. Claiborne, requesting military aid because of fears of a slave revolt.
Territorial Papers of the US - volume: 9 page: 327
Allard,   Orleans Territory, New Orleans
Allard, Male
Characterization of New Orleans residents, 1 July 1804
Territorial Papers of the US - volume: 9 page: 250
Allard, Senr   Orleans Territory, New Orleans
Allard, Senr   Male **Job:**   Planter
Characterization of New Orleans residents, 1 July 1804
Territorial Papers of the US - volume: 9 page: 253
Amelung, F. L.E.,   Orleans Territory, New Orleans
Amelung, F. L.E.,   Male **Job:** Merchant
Memorial to Congress from merchants of New Orleans, 9 Jan 1804, offering allegiance to the US
Territorial Papers of the US - volume: 9 page: 158
Andres, Joseph,   Orleans Territory
Andres, Joseph,   Male
Petition, 9 Nov 1804, by inhabitants of Pointe Coupee to Gov. Claiborne, requesting military aid because of fears of a slave revolt.

Territorial Papers of the US - volume: 9 page: 327
Arellery, Joseph,   Orleans Territory
Arellery, Joseph,   Male
Petition, 9 Nov 1804, by inhabitants of Pointe Coupee to Gov. Claiborne, requesting military aid because of fears of a slave revolt.
Territorial Papers of the US - volume: 9 page: 327
Argoti,   Orleans Territory, New Orleans
Argoti, Male
Characterization of New Orleans residents, 1 July 1804
Territorial Papers of the US - volume: 9 page: 251
Argoti, Antonio,   Orleans Territory, New Orleans
Argoti, Antonio,   Male **Job:** Municipality Head
"formerly a clerk & attorney"
Characterization of New Orleans residents, 1 July 1804
Territorial Papers of the US - volume: 9 page: 254
Auguste, Jacque,   Orleans Territory
Auguste, Jacque,   Male **Color:** Colored
Address from the free people of color Jan. 1804, volunteering for military service
Territorial Papers of the US - volume: 9 page: 175
Auguste, Philippe,   Orleans Territory
Auguste, Philippe,   Male **Color:** Colored
Address from the free people of color Jan. 1804, volunteering for military service
Territorial Papers of the US - volume: 9 page: 175
Auguste, Voltaire,   Orleans Territory
Auguste, Voltaire,   Male **Color:** Colored
Address from the free people of color Jan. 1804, volunteering for military service
Territorial Papers of the US - volume: 9 page: 175
Aurit, Louis,   Orleans Territory
Aurit, Louis,   Male **Color:** Colored
Address from the free people of color Jan. 1804, volunteering for military service
Territorial Papers of the US - volume: 9 page: 175
Babo, Pierre,   Orleans Territory
Babo, Pierre,   Male
Petition, 9 Nov 1804, by inhabitants of Pointe Coupee to Gov. Claiborne, requesting military aid because of fears of a slave revolt.
Territorial Papers of the US - volume: 9 page: 327
Bailly, Pierre, Orleans Territory

Bailly, Pierre, Male **Color:** Colored
"fils" [brother]
Address from the free people of color Jan. 1804,
volunteering for military service
Territorial Papers of the US - volume: 9 page: 175
Bailly, Pierre, Orleans Territory
Bailly, Pierre, Male **Color:** Colored
Address from the free people of color Jan. 1804,
volunteering for military service
Territorial Papers of the US - volume: 9 page: 175
Baker, Hilary, Orleans Territory, New Orleans
Baker, Hilary, Male
Recommendation, 1 Sept 1804, of William Brown
as Collector by the subscribers, merchants, traders,
and others of New Orleans
Territorial Papers of the US - volume: 9 page: 290
Banrepan, Noel, Orleans Territory
Banrepan, Noel, Male **Color:**
Colored
Address from the free people of color Jan. 1804,
volunteering for military service
Territorial Papers of the US - volume: 9 page: 174
Baron, Bte, Orleans Territory
Baron, Bte, Male
Petition, 9 Nov 1804, by inhabitants of Pointe
Coupee to Gov. Claiborne, requesting military aid
because of fears of a slave revolt.
Territorial Papers of the US - volume: 9 page: 327
Baru, Fcols, Orleans Territory
Baru, Fcols, Male
Petition, 9 Nov 1804, by inhabitants of Pointe
Coupee to Gov. Claiborne, requesting military aid
because of fears of a slave revolt.
Territorial Papers of the US - volume: 9 page: 327
Beauvais, At, Orleans Territory
Beauvais, At, Male
Petition, 9 Nov 1804, by inhabitants of Pointe
Coupee to Gov. Claiborne, requesting military aid
because of fears of a slave revolt.
Territorial Papers of the US - volume: 9 page: 327
Beauvais, Bte, Orleans Territory
Beauvais, Bte, Male
Petition, 9 Nov 1804, by inhabitants of Pointe
Coupee to Gov. Claiborne, requesting military aid
because of fears of a slave revolt.
Territorial Papers of the US - volume: 9 page: 327
Beauvais, Voc, Orleans Territory
Beauvais, Voc, Male

Petition, 9 Nov 1804, by inhabitants of Pointe
Coupee to Gov. Claiborne, requesting military aid
because of fears of a slave revolt.
Territorial Papers of the US - volume: 9 page: 327
Belanger, Francois, Orleans Territory
Belanger, Francois, Male
Petition, 9 Nov 1804, by inhabitants of Pointe
Coupee to Gov. Claiborne, requesting military aid
because of fears of a slave revolt.
Territorial Papers of the US - volume: 9 page: 326
Bellechasse, Colonel Orleans Territory, New
Orleans
Bellechasse, Colonel Male
"Commandant of the City Militia, formerly
a Spanish Officer, . . . A Creole of the Country,
unlettered"
Characterization of New Orleans residents, 1 July
1804
Territorial Papers of the US - volume: 9 page: 255
Bellechasse, Colonel Orleans Territory, New
Orleans
Bellechasse, Colonel Male
Persons recommended by Governor Claiborne for
members of the Legislative Council of the Orleans
Territory, 17 August 1804.
Territorial Papers of the US - volume: 9 page: 277
Bergeron, George, Orleans Territory
Bergeron, George, Male
Petition, 9 Nov 1804, by inhabitants of Pointe
Coupee to Gov. Claiborne, requesting military aid
because of fears of a slave revolt.
Territorial Papers of the US - volume: 9 page: 327
Bergeron, George, Orleans Territory
Bergeron, George, Male
Petition, 9 Nov 1804, by inhabitants of Pointe
Coupee to Gov. Claiborne, requesting military aid
because of fears of a slave revolt.
Territorial Papers of the US - volume: 9 page: 327
Bergeron, Louis, Orleans Territory
Bergeron, Louis, Male
Petition, 9 Nov 1804, by inhabitants of Pointe
Coupee to Gov. Claiborne, requesting military aid
because of fears of a slave revolt.
Territorial Papers of the US - volume: 9 page: 327
Bidetrenoulleau, Orleans Territory, New
Orleans
Bidetrenoulleau, Male
Petition, 17 Sep 1804, by inhabitants & colonists
of LA to Gov. Claiborne, requesting a commission
be established for fear of a slave revolt.

Territorial Papers of the US - volume: 9 page: 296
Bidou, Philippe,   Orleans Territory
        Bidou, Philippe,   Male
Petition, 9 Nov 1804, by inhabitants of Pointe Coupee to Gov. Claiborne, requesting military aid because of fears of a slave revolt.
Territorial Papers of the US - volume: 9 page: 327
Blanc, Marie, Orleans Territory, New Orleans
        Blanc, Marie,   Female
        "Agregee pour servir la communaute"
Ursuline Nuns to the President, 23 Apr 1804, seeking ratification of prior claim
Territorial Papers of the US - volume: 9 page: 232
Bocyfarree, Jn Bte,   Orleans Territory, New Orleans
        Bocyfarree, Jn Bte,   Male
Petition, 17 Sep 1804, by inhabitants & colonists of LA to Gov. Claiborne, requesting a commission be established for fear of a slave revolt.
Territorial Papers of the US - volume: 9 page: 296
Boidore, Charles,   Orleans Territory
        Boidore, Charles,   Male   **Color:** Colored
Address from the free people of color Jan. 1804, volunteering for military service
Territorial Papers of the US - volume: 9 page: 175
Bongaud,   Orleans Territory, New Orleans
        Bongaud,   Male   **Job:**   Merchant
        Business partner of Dejan
Memorial to Congress from merchants of New Orleans, 9 Jan 1804, offering allegiance to the US
Territorial Papers of the US - volume: 9 page: 158
Bonnett, Theod.,   Orleans Territory, New Orleans
        Bonnett, Theod,   Male
Recommendation, 1 Sept 1804, of William Brown as Collector by the subscribers, merchants, traders, and others of New Orleans
Territorial Papers of the US - volume: 9 page: 290
Boque or Poque, George,   Orleans Territory
        Boque or Poque, George,   Male
Petition, 9 Nov 1804, by inhabitants of Pointe Coupee to Gov. Claiborne, requesting military aid because of fears of a slave revolt.
Territorial Papers of the US - volume: 9 page: 327
Bore,   Orleans Territory, New Orleans
        Bore,   Male
Petition, 17 Sep 1804, by inhabitants & colonists of LA to Gov. Claiborne, requesting a commission be established for fear of a slave revolt.

Territorial Papers of the US - volume: 9 page: 296
Boree, Orleans Territory, New Orleans
        Boree, Male   **Job:**   Planter "rich"
Characterization of New Orleans residents, 1 July 1804
Territorial Papers of the US - volume: 9 page: 251
Boree, Orleans Territory, New Orleans
        Boree, Male   "of some fortune"
Characterization of New Orleans residents, 1 July 1804
Territorial Papers of the US - volume: 9 page: 248
Bores, Orleans Territory, New Orleans
        Bores, Male   **Job:**   Agriculturist
Characterization of New Orleans residents, 1 July 1804
Territorial Papers of the US - volume: 9 page: 254
Bosque, Batte, Orleans Territory, New Orleans
        Bosque, Batte, Male   **Job:**   Merchant
Memorial to Congress from merchants of New Orleans, 9 Jan 1804, offering allegiance to the US
Territorial Papers of the US - volume: 9 page: 158
Bougeat, Ve,   Orleans Territory
        Bougeat, Ve,   Male
Petition, 9 Nov 1804, by inhabitants of Pointe Coupee to Gov. Claiborne, requesting military aid because of fears of a slave revolt.
Territorial Papers of the US - volume: 9 page: 326
Bouligny, Dominique, Orleans Territory, New Orleans
        Bouligny, Dominique, Male   **Job:** Officer Father a planter
Characterization of New Orleans residents, 1 July 1804
Territorial Papers of the US - volume: 9 page: 254
Bourgeat, M,   Orleans Territory
        Bourgeat, M,   Male
Petition, 9 Nov 1804, by inhabitants of Pointe Coupee to Gov. Claiborne, requesting military aid because of fears of a slave revolt.
Territorial Papers of the US - volume: 9 page: 326
Bourgett, Zenon,   Orleans Territory
        Bourgett, Zenon,   Male
Petition, 9 Nov 1804, by inhabitants of Pointe Coupee to Gov. Claiborne, requesting military aid because of fears of a slave revolt.
Territorial Papers of the US - volume: 9 page: 327
Bouye, Pierre, Orleans Territory
        Bouye, Pierre, Male   **Color:** Colored
Address from the free people of color Jan. 1804, volunteering for military service

Territorial Papers of the US - volume: 9 page: 175
Bricou, Henry, Orleans Territory
Bricou, Henry, Male **Color:** Colored
Address from the free people of color Jan. 1804, volunteering for military service
Territorial Papers of the US - volume: 9 page: 174
Bringier, Tureaud, Orleans Territory, New Orleans
Bringier, Tureaud, Male **Job:** Merchant
Memorial to Congress from merchants of New Orleans, 9 Jan 1804, offering allegiance to the US
Territorial Papers of the US - volume: 9 page: 158
Brion, Louis, Orleans Territory
Brion, Louis, Male **Color:** Colored "fils" [son?]
Address from the free people of color Jan. 1804, volunteering for military service
Territorial Papers of the US - volume: 9 page: 175
Brown, Henry, Orleans Territory, New Orleans
Brown, Henry, Male **Job:** Notary Public Lawyer, late of the City of Washington
Letter, 30 Aug 1804, from Governor Claiborne to the President
Territorial Papers of the US - volume: 9 page: 286
Brown, Shepherd, Orleans Territory, New Orleans
Brown, Shepherd, Male & Co.
Recommendation, 1 Sept 1804, of William Brown as Collector by the subscribers, merchants, traders, and others of New Orleans
Territorial Papers of the US - volume: 9 page: 290
Brown, Shepherd, Orleans Territory, New Orleans
Brown, Shepherd, Male & Co.
Recommendation, 1 Sept 1804, of William Brown as Collector by the subscribers, merchants, traders, and others of New Orleans
Territorial Papers of the US - volume: 9 page: 290
Broyard, Etienne, Orleans Territory
Broyard, Etienne, Male
Petition, 9 Nov 1804, by inhabitants of Pointe Coupee to Gov. Claiborne, requesting military aid because of fears of a slave revolt.
Territorial Papers of the US - volume: 9 page: 327
Butler, Miner, Orleans Territory
Butler, Miner, Male

Petition, 9 Nov 1804, by inhabitants of Pointe Coupee to Gov. Claiborne, requesting military aid because of fears of a slave revolt.
Territorial Papers of the US - volume: 9 page: 326
Caillet, Jn, Orleans Territory, New Orleans
Caillet, Jn, Male
Petition, 17 Sep 1804, by inhabitants & colonists of LA to Gov. Claiborne, requesting a commission be established for fear of a slave revolt.
Territorial Papers of the US - volume: 9 page: 296
Caisergues, Orleans Territory, New Orleans
Caisergues, Male
Characterization of New Orleans residents, 1 July 1804
Territorial Papers of the US - volume: 9 page: 256
Cantarelle, Orleans Territory, New Orleans
Cantarelle, Male "Commandant of the German or Acadien Coast"
Characterization of New Orleans residents, 1 July 1804
Territorial Papers of the US - volume: 9 page: 255
Carraby, Ane, Orleans Territory, New Orleans
Carraby, Ane, Male **Job:** Merchant Business partner of Pre Carraby
Memorial to Congress from merchants of New Orleans, 9 Jan 1804, offering allegiance to the US
Territorial Papers of the US - volume: 9 page: 158
Carraby, Atne, Orleans Territory, New Orleans
Carraby, Atne, Male
Petition, 17 Sep 1804, by inhabitants & colonists of LA to Gov. Claiborne, requesting a commission be established for fear of a slave revolt.
Territorial Papers of the US - volume: 9 page: 296
Carraby, Pre, Orleans Territory, New Orleans
Carraby, Pre, Male **Job:** Merchant Business partner of Ane Carraby
Memorial to Congress from merchants of New Orleans, 9 Jan 1804, offering allegiance to the US
Territorial Papers of the US - volume: 9 page: 158
Carraby, Prre, Orleans Territory, New Orleans
Carraby, Prre, Male
Petition, 17 Sep 1804, by inhabitants & colonists of LA to Gov. Claiborne, requesting a commission be established for fear of a slave revolt.
Territorial Papers of the US - volume: 9 page: 296
Carrick, James, Orleans Territory, New Orleans
Carrick, James, Male

Recommendation, 1 Sept 1804, of William Brown as Collector by the subscribers, merchants, traders, and others of New Orleans
Territorial Papers of the US - volume: 9 page: 290
Cavelier,   Orleans Territory, New Orleans
        Cavelier,   Male   Partner   with brothers
Recommendation, 1 Sept 1804, of William Brown as Collector by the subscribers, merchants, traders, and others of New Orleans
Territorial Papers of the US - volume: 9 page: 290
Cavelier,   Orleans Territory, New Orleans
        Cavelier,   Male
Characterization of New Orleans residents, 1 July 1804
Territorial Papers of the US - volume: 9 page: 250
Cavelier,   Orleans Territory, New Orleans
        Cavelier,   Male   **Job:**   Merchant
        Business partner with brothers
Memorial to Congress from merchants of New Orleans, 9 Jan 1804, offering allegiance to the US
Territorial Papers of the US - volume: 9 page: 158
Cavelier, junr   Orleans Territory, New Orleans
        Cavelier, junr   Male
Characterization of New Orleans residents, 1 July 1804
Territorial Papers of the US - volume: 9 page: 253
Cavelier, Antne,   Orleans Territory, New Orleans
        Cavelier, Antne,   Male
Petition, 17 Sep 1804, by inhabitants & colonists of LA to Gov. Claiborne, requesting a commission be established for fear of a slave revolt.
Territorial Papers of the US - volume: 9 page: 296
Caves, Fransoi,   Orleans Territory
        Caves, Fransoi, Male   **Color:** Colored
        "pere" [father?]
Address from the free people of color Jan. 1804, volunteering for military service
Territorial Papers of the US - volume: 9 page: 174
Caxeux, Charle,   Orleans Territory
        Caxeux, Charle,   Male   **Color:** Colored
Address from the free people of color Jan. 1804, volunteering for military service
Territorial Papers of the US - volume: 9 page: 174
Cenas, B,   Orleans Territory, New Orleans
        Cenas, B,   Male

Recommendation, 1 Sept 1804, of William Brown as Collector by the subscribers, merchants, traders, and others of New Orleans
Territorial Papers of the US - volume: 9 page: 290
Cenas, P,   Orleans Territory, New Orleans
        Cenas, P,   Male
Recommendation, 1 Sept 1804, of William Brown as Collector by the subscribers, merchants, traders, and others of New Orleans
Territorial Papers of the US - volume: 9 page: 290
Cennois, Jean, Orleans Territory
        Cennois, Jean, Male   **Color:** Colored
Address from the free people of color Jan. 1804, volunteering for military service
Territorial Papers of the US - volume: 9 page: 175
Ceysergues,   Orleans Territory, New Orleans
        Ceysergues,   Male
Characterization of New Orleans residents, 1 July 1804
Territorial Papers of the US - volume: 9 page: 256
Charbonnet, L.,   Orleans   Territory,   New Orleans
        Charbonnet, L., Male
Petition, 17 Sep 1804, by inhabitants & colonists of LA to Gov. Claiborne, requesting a commission be established for fear of a slave revolt.
Territorial Papers of the US - volume: 9 page: 296
Charle, Jathainte,   Orleans Territory
        Charle, Jathainte,   Male   **Color:** Colored
Address from the free people of color Jan. 1804, volunteering for military service
Territorial Papers of the US - volume: 9 page: 175
Chesse, Fr,   Orleans Territory
        Chesse, Fr,   Male
Petition, 9 Nov 1804, by inhabitants of Pointe Coupee to Gov. Claiborne, requesting military aid because of fears of a slave revolt.
Territorial Papers of the US - volume: 9 page: 327
Chew, Orleans Territory, New Orleans
        Chew, Male   Partner of Relf
Recommendation, 1 Sept 1804, of William Brown as Collector by the subscribers, merchants, traders, and others of New Orleans
Territorial Papers of the US - volume: 9 page: 290
Chew, Orleans Territory, New Orleans
        Chew, Male   **Job:**   Merchant
        Business partner of Relf
Memorial to Congress from merchants of New Orleans, 9 Jan 1804, offering allegiance to the US

Territorial Papers of the US - volume: 9 page: 158
Chew, Beverly,   Orleans Territory, New Orleans
        Chew, Beverly, Male   "of   Virginia connected with M. D. Clark, . . . has served Gover Claiborne"
Characterization of New Orleans residents, 1 July 1804
Territorial Papers of the US - volume: 9 page: 256
Chiapella, Gha,   Orleans Territory, New Orleans
        Chiapella, Gha, Male   **Job:**   Merchant
Memorial to Congress from merchants of New Orleans, 9 Jan 1804, offering allegiance to the US
Territorial Papers of the US - volume: 9 page: 158
Chiapella, Jerome,   Orleans Territory, New Orleans
        Chiapella, Jerome,   Male   **Job:**   Merchant   **Born in:**   Genoa
Characterization of New Orleans residents, 1 July 1804
Territorial Papers of the US - volume: 9 page: 253
Chiappella,   Orleans Territory, New Orleans
        Chiappella,   Male   "rich"
Characterization of New Orleans residents, 1 July 1804
Territorial Papers of the US - volume: 9 page: 250
Clark, D.,   Orleans Territory, New Orleans
        Clark, D.,   Male
Characterization of New Orleans residents, 1 July 1804
Territorial Papers of the US - volume: 9 page: 255
Clark, Daniel, Orleans Territory, New Orleans
        Clark, Daniel, Male   **Job:**   Merchant
Memorial to Congress from merchants of New Orleans, 9 Jan 1804, offering allegiance to the US
Territorial Papers of the US - volume: 9 page: 158
Clay, John,   Orleans Territory, New Orleans
        Clay, John,   Male
Recommendation, 1 Sept 1804, of William Brown as Collector by the subscribers, merchants, traders, and others of New Orleans
Territorial Papers of the US - volume: 9 page: 290
Clouet,   Orleans Territory, New Orleans
        Clouet, Male   "a   younger   brother", "rich"
Characterization of New Orleans residents, 1 July 1804
Territorial Papers of the US - volume: 9 page: 250

Collins, Theophilus,   Orleans   Territory,   St. Landry
        Collins, Theophilus,   Male
        "American of wealth"
Persons recommended by Governor Claiborne for members of the Legislative Council of the Orleans Territory, 17 August 1804.
Territorial Papers of the US - volume: 9 page: 277
Commagere, Pre,   Orleans   Territory,   New Orleans
        Commagere, Pre,   Male   **Job:**   Merchant
Memorial to Congress from merchants of New Orleans, 9 Jan 1804, offering allegiance to the US
Territorial Papers of the US - volume: 9 page: 158
Croizet,   Orleans Territory
        Croizet,   Male
Petition, 9 Nov 1804, by inhabitants of Pointe Coupee to Gov. Claiborne, requesting military aid because of fears of a slave revolt.
Territorial Papers of the US - volume: 9 page: 326
Cuisergue,   Orleans Territory, New Orleans
        Cuisergue,   Male   **Job:**   Retired Merchant
Characterization of New Orleans residents, 1 July 1804
Territorial Papers of the US - volume: 9 page: 253
Cuitergue,   Orleans Territory, New Orleans
        Cuitergue,   Male
Characterization of New Orleans residents, 1 July 1804
Territorial Papers of the US - volume: 9 page: 250
D aigles, Baptiste,   Orleans Territory
        D aigles, Baptiste,   Male   **Color:**   Colored
Address from the free people of color Jan. 1804, volunteering for military service
Territorial Papers of the US - volume: 9 page: 175
Daunoy, Louis,   Orleans Territory
        Daunoy, Louis, Male   **Color:** Colored
        "fils" [brother?}
Address from the free people of color Jan. 1804, volunteering for military service
Territorial Papers of the US - volume: 9 page: 175
David "fils", Louis,   Orleans Territory
        David "fils", Louis,   Male
Petition, 9 Nov 1804, by inhabitants of Pointe Coupee to Gov. Claiborne, requesting military aid because of fears of a slave revolt.
Territorial Papers of the US - volume: 9 page: 327

David, Louis, Orleans Territory
David, Louis, Male
Petition, 9 Nov 1804, by inhabitants of Pointe Coupee to Gov. Claiborne, requesting military aid because of fears of a slave revolt.
Territorial Papers of the US - volume: 9 page: 327
David, Simon, Orleans Territory
David, Simon, Male
Petition, 9 Nov 1804, by inhabitants of Pointe Coupee to Gov. Claiborne, requesting military aid because of fears of a slave revolt.
Territorial Papers of the US - volume: 9 page: 327
Davis, S. B., Orleans Territory, New Orleans
Davis, S. B., Male
Recommendation, 1 Sept 1804, of William Brown as Collector by the subscribers, merchants, traders, and others of New Orleans
Territorial Papers of the US - volume: 9 page: 290
de Clouet, Brugny, Orleans Territory, New Orleans
de Clouet, Brugny, Male "Rich Creole"
Characterization of New Orleans residents, 1 July 1804
Territorial Papers of the US - volume: 9 page: 252
De La Hogue, Orleans Territory, New Orleans
De La Hogue, Male
Characterization of New Orleans residents, 1 July 1804
Territorial Papers of the US - volume: 9 page: 251
De La Hogue, J. M.B., Orleans Territory, New Orleans
De La Hogue, J. M.B., Male
Characterization of New Orleans residents, 1 July 1804
Territorial Papers of the US - volume: 9 page: 254
De Villeneuve, Orleans Territory
De Villeneuve, Male
Petition, 9 Nov 1804, by inhabitants of Pointe Coupee to Gov. Claiborne, requesting military aid because of fears of a slave revolt.
Territorial Papers of the US - volume: 9 page: 327
Debuis, Gaspard, Orleans Territory, New Orleans
Debuis, Gaspard, Male **Job:** Merchant "Magistrate"
Characterization of New Orleans residents, 1 July 1804
Territorial Papers of the US - volume: 9 page: 254

Debuis, Gaspard, Orleans Territory, New Orleans
Debuis, Gaspard, Male **Job:** Judge
Characterization of New Orleans residents, 1 July 1804
Territorial Papers of the US - volume: 9 page: 254
Debuys, Orleans Territory, New Orleans
Debuys, Male **Job:** Merchant
Characterization of New Orleans residents, 1 July 1804
Territorial Papers of the US - volume: 9 page: 251
Debuys, G., Orleans Territory, New Orleans
Debuys, G., Male **Job:** Merchant
Memorial to Congress from merchants of New Orleans, 9 Jan 1804, offering allegiance to the US
Territorial Papers of the US - volume: 9 page: 158
Declouits, B., Orleans Territory, New Orleans
Declouits, B., Male
Characterization of New Orleans residents, 1 July 1804
Territorial Papers of the US - volume: 9 page: 256
D'ecoup, Charles, Orleans Territory
D'ecoup, Charles, Male **Color:** Colored
Address from the free people of color Jan. 1804, volunteering for military service
Territorial Papers of the US - volume: 9 page: 175
Decour, Orleans Territory
Decour, Male
Petition, 9 Nov 1804, by inhabitants of Pointe Coupee to Gov. Claiborne, requesting military aid because of fears of a slave revolt.
Territorial Papers of the US - volume: 9 page: 327
Decour, H, Orleans Territory
Decour, H, Male
Petition, 9 Nov 1804, by inhabitants of Pointe Coupee to Gov. Claiborne, requesting military aid because of fears of a slave revolt.
Territorial Papers of the US - volume: 9 page: 327
Decour, Jn, Orleans Territory
Decour, Jn, Male
Petition, 9 Nov 1804, by inhabitants of Pointe Coupee to Gov. Claiborne, requesting military aid because of fears of a slave revolt.
Territorial Papers of the US - volume: 9 page: 327
Decoux, Valleri, Orleans Territory
Decoux, Valleri, Male
Petition, 9 Nov 1804, by inhabitants of Pointe

Coupee to Gov. Claiborne, requesting military aid because of fears of a slave revolt.
Territorial Papers of the US - volume: 9 page: 327
Decuir,   Orleans Territory
        Decuir, Male
Petition, 9 Nov 1804, by inhabitants of Pointe Coupee to Gov. Claiborne, requesting military aid because of fears of a slave revolt.
Territorial Papers of the US - volume: 9 page: 327
Decuir, Jh,   Orleans Territory
        Decuir, Jh,   Male
Petition, 9 Nov 1804, by inhabitants of Pointe Coupee to Gov. Claiborne, requesting military aid because of fears of a slave revolt.
Territorial Papers of the US - volume: 9 page: 327
Decuir, Jh.,   Orleans Territory
        Decuir, Jh.,   Male
Petition, 9 Nov 1804, by inhabitants of Pointe Coupee to Gov. Claiborne, requesting military aid because of fears of a slave revolt.
Territorial Papers of the US - volume: 9 page: 326
Decuir, Pierre,   Orleans Territory
        Decuir, Pierre, Male
Petition, 9 Nov 1804, by inhabitants of Pointe Coupee to Gov. Claiborne, requesting military aid because of fears of a slave revolt.
Territorial Papers of the US - volume: 9 page: 327
Dejan, Orleans Territory, New Orleans
        Dejan, Male   **Job:**   Merchant
        Business partner of Bongaud
Memorial to Congress from merchants of New Orleans, 9 Jan 1804, offering allegiance to the US
Territorial Papers of the US - volume: 9 page: 158
Demasiliere, Eugene,   Orleans Territory
        Demasiliere, Eugene,   Male   **Color:** Colored
Address from the free people of color Jan. 1804, volunteering for military service
Territorial Papers of the US - volume: 9 page: 175
Demazelliere, Baltazard,   Orleans Territory
        Demazelliere, Baltazard,   Male
        Color: Colored
Address from the free people of color Jan. 1804, volunteering for military service
Territorial Papers of the US - volume: 9 page: 174
Demouche, Batiste,   Orleans Territory
        Demouche, Batiste,   Male
Petition, 9 Nov 1804, by inhabitants of Pointe Coupee to Gov. Claiborne, requesting military aid because of fears of a slave revolt.

Territorial Papers of the US - volume: 9 page: 327
Demouche, Francois,   Orleans Territory
        Demouche, Francois,   Male
Petition, 9 Nov 1804, by inhabitants of Pointe Coupee to Gov. Claiborne, requesting military aid because of fears of a slave revolt.
Territorial Papers of the US - volume: 9 page: 327
Depres, Jn Bte,   Orleans Territory
        Depres, Jn Bte, Male   **Color:** Colored
Address from the free people of color Jan. 1804, volunteering for military service
Territorial Papers of the US - volume: 9 page: 174
Derbigny,   Orleans Territory, New Orleans
        Derbigny,   Male   "young man"
Characterization of New Orleans residents, 1 July 1804
Territorial Papers of the US - volume: 9 page: 251
Derbigny,   Orleans Territory, New Orleans
        Derbigny,   Male   **Born   in:** France
Characterization of New Orleans residents, 1 July 1804
Territorial Papers of the US - volume: 9 page: 257
Derbigny, Pre, Orleans Territory, New Orleans
        Derbigny, Pre, Male   **Job:**   Clerk of the court
Characterization of New Orleans residents, 1 July 1804
Territorial Papers of the US - volume: 9 page: 254
Dervigneux, J.,   Orleans Territory, New Orleans
        Dervigneux, J., Male
Petition, 17 Sep 1804, by inhabitants & colonists of LA to Gov. Claiborne, requesting a commission be established for fear of a slave revolt.
Territorial Papers of the US - volume: 9 page: 296
Desilets,   Orleans Territory, New Orleans
        Desilets,   Male
Characterization of New Orleans residents, 1 July 1804
Territorial Papers of the US - volume: 9 page: 254
Detrehan,   Orleans Territory, New Orleans
        Detrehan,   Male   "rich"
Characterization of New Orleans residents, 1 July 1804
Territorial Papers of the US - volume: 9 page: 249
Detrehan,   Orleans Territory, New Orleans
        Detrehan,   Male   **Job:**   Planter
        "Rich"

Characterization of New Orleans residents, 1 July 1804

Territorial Papers of the US - volume: 9 page: 252

Detrehan, Orleans Territory, New Orleans

Detrehan, Male "a native Frenchman in politics & affections, was one of the tools of M. Laussat"

Characterization of New Orleans residents, 1 July 1804

Territorial Papers of the US - volume: 9 page: 257

Detrihan, Orleans Territory, New Orleans

Detrihan, Male

Characterization of New Orleans residents, 1 July 1804

Territorial Papers of the US - volume: 9 page: 254

Dheberont, Orleans Territory, New Orleans

Dheberont, Male **Job:** School Master "formerly an officer in French Service'

Characterization of New Orleans residents, 1 July 1804

Territorial Papers of the US - volume: 9 page: 253

Dolliote, Jn Louis, Orleans Territory

Dolliote, Jn Louis, Male **Color:** Colored

Address from the free people of color Jan. 1804, volunteering for military service

Territorial Papers of the US - volume: 9 page: 175

Donaldson, William, Orleans Territory, New Orleans

Donaldson, William, Male **Job:** Merchant **Born in:** England

Persons recommended by Governor Claiborne for members of the Legislative Council of the Orleans Territory, 17 August 1804.

Territorial Papers of the US - volume: 9 page: 277

D'orgenoi, Le Breton, Orleans Territory, New Orleans

D'orgenoi, Le Breton, Male **Job:** Planter "French Creole"

Persons recommended by Governor Claiborne for members of the Legislative Council of the Orleans Territory, 17 August 1804.

Territorial Papers of the US - volume: 9 page: 277

D'orgenois, Le Breton, Orleans Territory, New Orleans

D'orgenois, Le Breton, Male

Characterization of New Orleans residents, 1 July 1804

Territorial Papers of the US - volume: 9 page: 256

Dorgenoy, Fs jh Le Breton, Orleans Territory, New Orleans

Dorgenoy, Fs jh Le Breton, Male

Petition, 17 Sep 1804, by inhabitants & colonists of LA to Gov. Claiborne, requesting a commission be established for fear of a slave revolt.

Territorial Papers of the US - volume: 9 page: 296

Dorsiere, Orleans Territory, New Orleans

Dorsiere, Male **Job:** Merchant **Born in:** Switzerland

Characterization of New Orleans residents, 1 July 1804

Territorial Papers of the US - volume: 9 page: 252

Dorsiere, Orleans Territory, New Orleans

Dorsiere, Male

Characterization of New Orleans residents, 1 July 1804

Territorial Papers of the US - volume: 9 page: 249

D'orsiere, Euge, Orleans Territory, New Orleans

D'orsiere, Euge, Male

Recommendation, 1 Sept 1804, of William Brown as Collector by the subscribers, merchants, traders, and others of New Orleans

Territorial Papers of the US - volume: 9 page: 290

Dorsiere, Euge, Orleans Territory, New Orleans

Dorsiere, Euge, Male **Job:** Merchant

Memorial to Congress from merchants of New Orleans, 9 Jan 1804, offering allegiance to the US

Territorial Papers of the US - volume: 9 page: 158

Dorsierere, Eugene, Orleans Territory, New Orleans

Dorsierere, Eugene, Male **Job:** Judge

Characterization of New Orleans residents, 1 July 1804

Territorial Papers of the US - volume: 9 page: 254

Dorsieres, Orleans Territory, New Orleans

Dorsieres, Male "formerly a dancing master in Philadelphia"

Characterization of New Orleans residents, 1 July 1804

Territorial Papers of the US - volume: 9 page: 255

Dow, Orleans Territory, New Orleans

Dow, Male **Job:** Doctor "a Scotch Man, of about thirty years residence in the Province"

Characterization of New Orleans residents, 1 July 1804

Territorial Papers of the US - volume: 9 page: 255
Dow, Robert,   Orleans Territory, New Orleans
Dow, Robert, Male **Job:** Doctor
"Native of Scotland; many years established in this country"
Persons recommended by Governor Claiborne for members of the Legislative Council of the Orleans Territory, 17 August 1804.
Territorial Papers of the US - volume: 9 page: 277
DuBourg, P. F., Jr   Orleans Territory, New Orleans
DuBourg, P. F., Jr   Male **Job:** Merchant
Memorial to Congress from merchants of New Orleans, 9 Jan 1804, offering allegiance to the US
Territorial Papers of the US - volume: 9 page: 158
DuBourg, P. F., Jr   Orleans Territory, New Orleans
DuBourg, P. F., Jr   Male
Recommendation, 1 Sept 1804, of William Brown as Collector by the subscribers, merchants, traders, and others of New Orleans
Territorial Papers of the US - volume: 9 page: 290
Dubuche, Messr   Orleans Territory, Attakapas
Dubuche, Messr   Male **Job:** French planter
Persons recommended by Governor Claiborne for members of the Legislative Council of the Orleans Territory, 17 August 1804.
Territorial Papers of the US - volume: 9 page: 278
Ducouneaux,   Orleans Territory, New Orleans
Ducouneaux,   Male
Characterization of New Orleans residents, 1 July 1804
Territorial Papers of the US - volume: 9 page: 251
Ducourneaux,   Orleans Territory, New Orleans
Ducourneaux, Male **Job:** Planter
Characterization of New Orleans residents, 1 July 1804
Territorial Papers of the US - volume: 9 page: 254
Ducret, Barthelemi,   Orleans Territory
Ducret, Barthelemi, Male **Color:** Colored
Address from the free people of color Jan. 1804, volunteering for military service
Territorial Papers of the US - volume: 9 page: 174
Dufan, C B,   Orleans Territory, New Orleans
Dufan, C B,   Male

Petition, 17 Sep 1804, by inhabitants & colonists of LA to Gov. Claiborne, requesting a commission be established for fear of a slave revolt.
Territorial Papers of the US - volume: 9 page: 296
Dufan, C. B.,   Orleans Territory, New Orleans
Dufan, C. B.,   Male
Recommendation, 1 Sept 1804, of William Brown as Collector by the subscribers, merchants, traders, and others of New Orleans
Territorial Papers of the US - volume: 9 page: 290
Dufourd "Pere", Charles,   Orleans Territory
Dufourd "Pere", Charles,   Male
Petition, 9 Nov 1804, by inhabitants of Pointe Coupee to Gov. Claiborne, requesting military aid because of fears of a slave revolt.
Territorial Papers of the US - volume: 9 page: 327
Duplantier,   Orleans Territory, New Orleans
Duplantier,   Male "of Batton Rouge, rich"
Characterization of New Orleans residents, 1 July 1804
Territorial Papers of the US - volume: 9 page: 255
Duplessis,   Orleans Territory, New Orleans
Duplessis,   Male **Job:** Business
Characterization of New Orleans residents, 1 July 1804
Territorial Papers of the US - volume: 9 page: 250
Duplessis, F.,   Orleans Territory, New Orleans
Duplessis, F.,   Male **Job:** Merchant
Memorial to Congress from merchants of New Orleans, 9 Jan 1804, offering allegiance to the US
Territorial Papers of the US - volume: 9 page: 158
Duplessis, F.,   Orleans Territory, New Orleans
Duplessis, F.,   Male
Recommendation, 1 Sept 1804, of William Brown as Collector by the subscribers, merchants, traders, and others of New Orleans
Territorial Papers of the US - volume: 9 page: 290
Duplessis, Francis,   Orleans Territory, New Orleans
Duplessis, Francis,   Male
Characterization of New Orleans residents, 1 July 1804
Territorial Papers of the US - volume: 9 page: 253
Duplessis, Francis,   Orleans Territory, New Orleans
Duplessis, Francis,   Male **Job:** French merchant
Persons recommended by Governor Claiborne for

members of the Legislative Council of the Orleans Territory, 17 August 1804.
Territorial Papers of the US - volume: 9 page: 278
Durall, Messr Orleans Territory, Attakapas
Durall, Messr   Male   **Job:**   French planter
Persons recommended by Governor Claiborne for members of the Legislative Council of the Orleans Territory, 17 August 1804.
Territorial Papers of the US - volume: 9 page: 278
Durant, Jean Marie, Orleans Territory
Durant, Jean Marie,   Male
Petition, 9 Nov 1804, by inhabitants of Pointe Coupee to Gov. Claiborne, requesting military aid because of fears of a slave revolt.
Territorial Papers of the US - volume: 9 page: 327
Duret, Bte,   Orleans Territory, New Orleans
Duret, Bte,   Male
Petition, 17 Sep 1804, by inhabitants & colonists of LA to Gov. Claiborne, requesting a commission be established for fear of a slave revolt.
Territorial Papers of the US - volume: 9 page: 296
Durnford, Thos,   Orleans Territory, New Orleans
Durnford, Thos,   Male
Recommendation, 1 Sept 1804, of William Brown as Collector by the subscribers, merchants, traders, and others of New Orleans
Territorial Papers of the US - volume: 9 page: 290
Dusser, Jn Fs, Orleans Territory, New Orleans
Dusser, Jn Fs,   Male   **Job:**   Merchant
Memorial to Congress from merchants of New Orleans, 9 Jan 1804, offering allegiance to the US
Territorial Papers of the US - volume: 9 page: 158
Earle, Orleans Territory, New Orleans
Earle,   Male   Partner of Jones & Co.
Recommendation, 1 Sept 1804, of William Brown as Collector by the subscribers, merchants, traders, and others of New Orleans
Territorial Papers of the US - volume: 9 page: 290
Elloy, St,   Orleans Territory
Elloy, St,   Male
Petition, 9 Nov 1804, by inhabitants of Pointe Coupee to Gov. Claiborne, requesting military aid because of fears of a slave revolt.
Territorial Papers of the US - volume: 9 page: 327
Emery,   Orleans Territory, New Orleans
Emery, Male   "Not in New Orleans"
Characterization of New Orleans residents, 1 July 1804
Territorial Papers of the US - volume: 9 page: 251
Emory,   Orleans Territory, New Orleans
Emory, Male
Characterization of New Orleans residents, 1 July 1804
Territorial Papers of the US - volume: 9 page: 254
Evins, Whitton,   Orleans Territory, New Orleans
Evins, Whitton,   Male
Recommendation, 1 Sept 1804, of William Brown as Collector by the subscribers, merchants, traders, and others of New Orleans
Territorial Papers of the US - volume: 9 page: 290
Fabre "pere", Jaque, Orleans Territory
Fabre "pere", Jaque,   Male
Petition, 9 Nov 1804, by inhabitants of Pointe Coupee to Gov. Claiborne, requesting military aid because of fears of a slave revolt.
Territorial Papers of the US - volume: 9 page: 327
Fabre, Joseph, Orleans Territory
Fabre, Joseph,   Male   "De L age la vigeur, Jai fai la rigeur y ache chate"
Petition, 9 Nov 1804, by inhabitants of Pointe Coupee to Gov. Claiborne, requesting military aid because of fears of a slave revolt.
Territorial Papers of the US - volume: 9 page: 327
Fabre, Z.,   Orleans Territory
Fabre, Z.,   Male
Petition, 9 Nov 1804, by inhabitants of Pointe Coupee to Gov. Claiborne, requesting military aid because of fears of a slave revolt.
Territorial Papers of the US - volume: 9 page: 327
Farrell, J. B., Orleans Territory, New Orleans
Farrell, J. B.,   Male   **Job:**   Merchant
Business Partner of H. O'Hara
Memorial to Congress from merchants of New Orleans, 9 Jan 1804, offering allegiance to the US
Territorial Papers of the US - volume: 9 page: 158
Farrell, J.B., Orleans Territory, New Orleans
Farrell, J.B.,   Male   Partner   of   H. O'Hara
Recommendation, 1 Sept 1804, of William Brown as Collector by the subscribers, merchants, traders, and others of New Orleans
Territorial Papers of the US - volume: 9 page: 290
Faurie,   Orleans Territory, New Orleans
Faurie, Male
Characterization of New Orleans residents, 1 July 1804
Territorial Papers of the US - volume: 9 page: 254

Faurie,   Orleans Territory, New Orleans
         Faurie, Male   **Job:**   Merchant
Characterization of New Orleans residents, 1 July 1804
Territorial Papers of the US - volume: 9 page: 252
Faurie,   Orleans Territory, New Orleans
         Faurie, Male   "of polished education"
Characterization of New Orleans residents, 1 July 1804
Territorial Papers of the US - volume: 9 page: 256
Faurie,   Orleans Territory, New Orleans
         Faurie, Male   **Job:**   Merchant
Characterization of New Orleans residents, 1 July 1804
Territorial Papers of the US - volume: 9 page: 249
Faurie, Jh,   Orleans Territory, New Orleans
         Faurie, Jh,   Male   **Job:**   Merchant
Memorial to Congress from merchants of New Orleans, 9 Jan 1804, offering allegiance to the US
Territorial Papers of the US - volume: 9 page: 158
Faurie, Jh,   Orleans Territory, New Orleans
         Faurie, Jh,   Male
Petition, 17 Sep 1804, by inhabitants & colonists of LA to Gov. Claiborne, requesting a commission be established for fear of a slave revolt.
Territorial Papers of the US - volume: 9 page: 296
Faurie, Jh,   Orleans Territory, New Orleans
         Faurie, Jh,   Male
Recommendation, 1 Sept 1804, of William Brown as Collector by the subscribers, merchants, traders, and others of New Orleans
Territorial Papers of the US - volume: 9 page: 290
Favre, Geo. F.,   Orleans Territory, New Orleans
         Favre, Geo. F., Male   **Job:**   Merchant
Memorial to Congress from merchants of New Orleans, 9 Jan 1804, offering allegiance to the US
Territorial Papers of the US - volume: 9 page: 158
Ferdinand, Louis,   Orleans Territory
         Ferdinand, Louis,   Male   **Color:**   Colored
Address from the free people of color Jan. 1804, volunteering for military service
Territorial Papers of the US - volume: 9 page: 175
Flood, William,   Orleans Territory, New Orleans
         Flood, William,   Male
Recommendation, 1 Sept 1804, of William Brown as Collector by the subscribers, merchants, traders, and others of New Orleans

Territorial Papers of the US - volume: 9 page: 290
Fonvergne, Voltairre, Orleans Territory
         Fonvergne, Voltairre,   Male   **Color:**   Colored
Address from the free people of color Jan. 1804, volunteering for military service
Territorial Papers of the US - volume: 9 page: 174
Fortier,   Orleans Territory, New Orleans
         Fortier, Male   'Rich"
Characterization of New Orleans residents, 1 July 1804
Territorial Papers of the US - volume: 9 page: 250
Fortier, M.,   Orleans Territory, New Orleans
         Fortier, M.,   Male   In business with son
Recommendation, 1 Sept 1804, of William Brown as Collector by the subscribers, merchants, traders, and others of New Orleans
Territorial Papers of the US - volume: 9 page: 290
Fortier, Michael,   Orleans Territory, New Orleans
         Fortier, Michael,   Male   **Job:**   Merchant   "Rich Creole"
Characterization of New Orleans residents, 1 July 1804
Territorial Papers of the US - volume: 9 page: 252
Fortier, Ml,   Orleans Territory, New Orleans
         Fortier, Ml,   Male
Petition, 17 Sep 1804, by inhabitants & colonists of LA to Gov. Claiborne, requesting a commission be established for fear of a slave revolt.
Territorial Papers of the US - volume: 9 page: 296
Fortier, Ml,   Orleans Territory, New Orleans
         Fortier, Ml,   Male   **Job:**   Merchant
Memorial to Congress from merchants of New Orleans, 9 Jan 1804, offering allegiance to the US
Territorial Papers of the US - volume: 9 page: 158
Fortier, Nobert,   Orleans Territory
         Fortier, Nobert, Male   **Color:**   Colored
Address from the free people of color Jan. 1804, volunteering for military service
Territorial Papers of the US - volume: 9 page: 175
Fortin, L.,   Orleans Territory, New Orleans
         Fortin, L.,   Male
Petition, 17 Sep 1804, by inhabitants & colonists of LA to Gov. Claiborne, requesting a commission be established for fear of a slave revolt.
Territorial Papers of the US - volume: 9 page: 296
Foucher, Aantoine,   Orleans Territory

Foucher, Aantoine,   Male **Color:** Colored
Address from the free people of color Jan. 1804, volunteering for military service
Territorial Papers of the US - volume: 9 page: 175
Foutenet, Messr   Orleans   Territory, Attakapas
Foutenet, Messr Male   **Job:**   French planter
Persons recommended by Governor Claiborne for members of the Legislative Council of the Orleans Territory, 17 August 1804.
Territorial Papers of the US - volume: 9 page: 278
Frechinet, Honoree,   Orleans Territory
Frechinet, Honoree,   Male   **Color:** Colored
Address from the free people of color Jan. 1804, volunteering for military service
Territorial Papers of the US - volume: 9 page: 175
Freret, James, Orleans Territory, New Orleans
Freret, James,   Male   **Job:**   Merchant
Memorial to Congress from merchants of New Orleans, 9 Jan 1804, offering allegiance to the US
Territorial Papers of the US - volume: 9 page: 158
Gaillard,   Orleans Territory, New Orleans
Gaillard,   Male   **Job:**   Merchant
Business partner of Jaure
Memorial to Congress from merchants of New Orleans, 9 Jan 1804, offering allegiance to the US
Territorial Papers of the US - volume: 9 page: 158
Gaillard,   Orleans Territory, New Orleans
Gaillard,   Male
Petition, 17 Sep 1804, by inhabitants & colonists of LA to Gov. Claiborne, requesting a commission be established for fear of a slave revolt.
Territorial Papers of the US - volume: 9 page: 296
Garidel,   Orleans Territory, New Orleans
Garidel,   Male
Petition, 17 Sep 1804, by inhabitants & colonists of LA to Gov. Claiborne, requesting a commission be established for fear of a slave revolt.
Territorial Papers of the US - volume: 9 page: 296
Garland, Wm G.,   Orleans Territory, New Orleans
Garland, Wm G.,   Male   **Job:** Merchant
Memorial to Congress from merchants of New Orleans, 9 Jan 1804, offering allegiance to the US
Territorial Papers of the US - volume: 9 page: 158

Garland, Wm G.,   Orleans Territory, New Orleans
Garland, Wm G.,   Male
Petition, 17 Sep 1804, by inhabitants & colonists of LA to Gov. Claiborne, requesting a commission be established for fear of a slave revolt.
Territorial Papers of the US - volume: 9 page: 296
Gelston,   Orleans Territory, New Orleans
Gelston,   Male   Partner   of Mumford
Recommendation, 1 Sept 1804, of William Brown as Collector by the subscribers, merchants, traders, and others of New Orleans
Territorial Papers of the US - volume: 9 page: 290
Genois, Bernard,   Orleans Territory, New Orleans
Genois, Bernard,   Male   **Job:** Merchant
Memorial to Congress from merchants of New Orleans, 9 Jan 1804, offering allegiance to the US
Territorial Papers of the US - volume: 9 page: 158
Geren, Guilliom,   Orleans Territory
Geren, Guilliom,   Male
Petition, 9 Nov 1804, by inhabitants of Pointe Coupee to Gov. Claiborne, requesting military aid because of fears of a slave revolt.
Territorial Papers of the US - volume: 9 page: 327
Girandeau,   Orleans Territory, New Orleans
Girandeau,   Male
Characterization of New Orleans residents, 1 July 1804
Territorial Papers of the US - volume: 9 page: 251
Girandeau,   Orleans Territory, New Orleans
Girandeau,   Male   **Job:**   Planter
Characterization of New Orleans residents, 1 July 1804
Territorial Papers of the US - volume: 9 page: 254
Gireaudeau, B.,   Orleans Territory, New Orleans
Gireaudeau, B., Male
Recommendation, 1 Sept 1804, of William Brown as Collector by the subscribers, merchants, traders, and others of New Orleans
Territorial Papers of the US - volume: 9 page: 290
Girod, Jn Fs, Orleans Territory, New Orleans
Girod, Jn Fs,   Male
Recommendation, 1 Sept 1804, of William Brown as Collector by the subscribers, merchants, traders, and others of New Orleans
Territorial Papers of the US - volume: 9 page: 290

Girod, Jn Fs,   Orleans Territory, New Orleans
Girod, Jn Fs,   Male   **Job:**   Merchant
Memorial to Congress from merchants of New Orleans, 9 Jan 1804, offering allegiance to the US
Territorial Papers of the US - volume: 9 page: 158
Girod, N.,   Orleans Territory, New Orleans
Girod, N.,   Male
Petition, 17 Sep 1804, by inhabitants & colonists of LA to Gov. Claiborne, requesting a commission be established for fear of a slave revolt.
Territorial Papers of the US - volume: 9 page: 296
Girod, N.,   Orleans Territory, New Orleans
Girod, N.,   Male
Recommendation, 1 Sept 1804, of William Brown as Collector by the subscribers, merchants, traders, and others of New Orleans
Territorial Papers of the US - volume: 9 page: 290
Girod, N.,   Orleans Territory, New Orleans
Girod, N.,   Male   **Job:**   Merchant
Business partner with brother
Memorial to Congress from merchants of New Orleans, 9 Jan 1804, offering allegiance to the US
Territorial Papers of the US - volume: 9 page: 158
Goseran, Cesere,   Orleans Territory
Goseran, Cesere,   Male
Petition, 9 Nov 1804, by inhabitants of Pointe Coupee to Gov. Claiborne, requesting military aid because of fears of a slave revolt.
Territorial Papers of the US - volume: 9 page: 327
Gotier, Guillomme,   Orleans Territory
Gotier, Guillomme,   Male
Petition, 9 Nov 1804, by inhabitants of Pointe Coupee to Gov. Claiborne, requesting military aid because of fears of a slave revolt.
Territorial Papers of the US - volume: 9 page: 327
Gougit,   Orleans Territory
Gougit,   Male
Petition, 9 Nov 1804, by inhabitants of Pointe Coupee to Gov. Claiborne, requesting military aid because of fears of a slave revolt.
Territorial Papers of the US - volume: 9 page: 327
Greffin, Stephen,   Orleans Territory, New Orleans
Greffin, Stephen,   Male
Recommendation, 1 Sept 1804, of William Brown as Collector by the subscribers, merchants, traders, and others of New Orleans
Territorial Papers of the US - volume: 9 page: 290
Gremillon,   Orleans Territory
Gremillon,   Male   "Gremillon fils"
Petition, 9 Nov 1804, by inhabitants of Pointe Coupee to Gov. Claiborne, requesting military aid because of fears of a slave revolt.
Territorial Papers of the US - volume: 9 page: 326
Gremillon, Charlot,   Orleans Territory
Gremillon, Charlot,   Male
Petition, 9 Nov 1804, by inhabitants of Pointe Coupee to Gov. Claiborne, requesting military aid because of fears of a slave revolt.
Territorial Papers of the US - volume: 9 page: 327
Guillot, Pierre a,   Orleans Territory, New Orleans
Guillot, Pierre a,   Male   "formerly a Gentleman in the French Service . . . naturalized & american Citizen"
Characterization of New Orleans residents, 1 July 1804
Territorial Papers of the US - volume: 9 page: 253
Guillot, Pre A,   Orleans Territory, New Orleans
Guillot, Pre A,   Male
Characterization of New Orleans residents, 1 July 1804
Territorial Papers of the US - volume: 9 page: 254
Guillote, Pierre a,   Orleans Territory, New Orleans
Guillote, Pierre a,   Male
Characterization of New Orleans residents, 1 July 1804
Territorial Papers of the US - volume: 9 page: 256
Gullote,   Orleans Territory, New Orleans
Gullote,   Male
Characterization of New Orleans residents, 1 July 1804
Territorial Papers of the US - volume: 9 page: 251
Gurley,   Orleans Territory, New Orleans
Gurley,   Male
Letter, 30 Aug 1804, from Governor Claiborne to the President [on pages 285-286]
Territorial Papers of the US - volume: 9 page: 285
Gurley, Jno W,   Orleans Territory, New Orleans
Gurley, Jno W,   Male
Recommendation, 1 Sept 1804, of William Brown as Collector by the subscribers, merchants, traders, and others of New Orleans
Territorial Papers of the US - volume: 9 page: 290
Hardy, Baptiste,   Orleans Territory
Hardy, Baptiste,   Male   **Color:**   Colored

Address from the free people of color Jan. 1804, volunteering for military service
Territorial Papers of the US - volume: 9 page: 175
Hardy, Joachim, Orleans Territory
Hardy, Joachim, Male **Color:** Colored
Address from the free people of color Jan. 1804, volunteering for military service
Territorial Papers of the US - volume: 9 page: 175
Hardy, Louis, Orleans Territory
Hardy, Louis, Male **Color:** Colored
Address from the free people of color Jan. 1804, volunteering for military service
Territorial Papers of the US - volume: 9 page: 175
Harman, Orleans Territory, New Orleans
Harman, Male Partner of Winter
Recommendation, 1 Sept 1804, of William Brown as Collector by the subscribers, merchants, traders, and others of New Orleans
Territorial Papers of the US - volume: 9 page: 290
Henderson, Orleans Territory, New Orleans
Henderson, Male **Job:** Merchant
Business partner of Kenner
Memorial to Congress from merchants of New Orleans, 9 Jan 1804, offering allegiance to the US
Territorial Papers of the US - volume: 9 page: 158
Henderson, Orleans Territory, New Orleans
Henderson, Male Partner of Kenner
Recommendation, 1 Sept 1804, of William Brown as Collector by the subscribers, merchants, traders, and others of New Orleans
Territorial Papers of the US - volume: 9 page: 290
Hernus, S., Orleans Territory
Hernus, S., Male
Petition, 9 Nov 1804, by inhabitants of Pointe Coupee to Gov. Claiborne, requesting military aid because of fears of a slave revolt.
Territorial Papers of the US - volume: 9 page: 327
Hes, Noel, Orleans Territory
Hes, Noel, Male **Color:** Colored
Address from the free people of color Jan. 1804, volunteering for military service
Territorial Papers of the US - volume: 9 page: 175
Holmes, Orleans Territory, New Orleans
Holmes, Male **Job:** Merchant
Business partner with Zackarie
Memorial to Congress from merchants of New Orleans, 9 Jan 1804, offering allegiance to the US
Territorial Papers of the US - volume: 9 page: 158
Holmes, Orleans Territory, New Orleans

Holmes, Male Partner of Zacharie
Recommendation, 1 Sept 1804, of William Brown as Collector by the subscribers, merchants, traders, and others of New Orleans
Territorial Papers of the US - volume: 9 page: 290
Hugont, Henry, Orleans Territory
Hugont, Henry, Male **Color:** Colored
Address from the free people of color Jan. 1804, volunteering for military service
Territorial Papers of the US - volume: 9 page: 175
Hulings, Wm E, Orleans Territory, New Orleans
Hulings, Wm E, Male **Job:** Merchant
Memorial to Congress from merchants of New Orleans, 9 Jan 1804, offering allegiance to the US
Territorial Papers of the US - volume: 9 page: 158
Jarreau, Bosemon, Orleans Territory
Jarreau, Bosemon, Male
Petition, 9 Nov 1804, by inhabitants of Pointe Coupee to Gov. Claiborne, requesting military aid because of fears of a slave revolt.
Territorial Papers of the US - volume: 9 page: 327
Jarreau, Celestin, Orleans Territory
Jarreau, Celestin, Male
Petition, 9 Nov 1804, by inhabitants of Pointe Coupee to Gov. Claiborne, requesting military aid because of fears of a slave revolt.
Territorial Papers of the US - volume: 9 page: 327
Jarreau, Joe, Orleans Territory
Jarreau, Joe, Male
Petition, 9 Nov 1804, by inhabitants of Pointe Coupee to Gov. Claiborne, requesting military aid because of fears of a slave revolt.
Territorial Papers of the US - volume: 9 page: 327
Jaure, Orleans Territory, New Orleans
Jaure, Male **Job:** Merchant
Business partner of Gaillard
Memorial to Congress from merchants of New Orleans, 9 Jan 1804, offering allegiance to the US
Territorial Papers of the US - volume: 9 page: 158
Jeune, Philippon, Orleans Territory, New Orleans
Jeune, Philippon, Male **Job:** Merchant
Memorial to Congress from merchants of New Orleans, 9 Jan 1804, offering allegiance to the US
Territorial Papers of the US - volume: 9 page: 158

Johnston, James, Orleans Territory, New Orleans
Johnston, James, Male **Job:** Merchant
Memorial to Congress from merchants of New Orleans, 9 Jan 1804, offering allegiance to the US
Territorial Papers of the US - volume: 9 page: 158
Jones, Orleans Territory, New Orleans
Jones, Male Partner of Earle & Co.
Recommendation, 1 Sept 1804, of William Brown as Collector by the subscribers, merchants, traders, and others of New Orleans
Territorial Papers of the US - volume: 9 page: 290
Jones, Clark, Orleans Territory, New Orleans
Jones, Clark, Male
Characterization of New Orleans residents, 1 July 1804
Territorial Papers of the US - volume: 9 page: 253
Jones, Evan, Orleans Territory, New Orleans
Jones, Evan, 65 Male "a man of education, an American by birth"
Characterization of New Orleans residents, 1 July 1804
Territorial Papers of the US - volume: 9 page: 255
Jones, Evan, Orleans Territory, New Orleans
Jones, Evan, Male **Job:** Merchant
Memorial to Congress from merchants of New Orleans, 9 Jan 1804, offering allegiance to the US
Territorial Papers of the US - volume: 9 page: 158
Jones, Evan, Orleans Territory, New Orleans
Jones, Evan, Male
Characterization of New Orleans residents, 1 July 1804
Territorial Papers of the US - volume: 9 page: 257
Jones, Evan, Orleans Territory, New Orleans
Jones, Evan, Male "resided 35 years at N. Orleans"
Characterization of New Orleans residents, 1 July 1804
Territorial Papers of the US - volume: 9 page: 258
Jounon, Orleans Territory
Jounon, Male
Petition, 9 Nov 1804, by inhabitants of Pointe Coupee to Gov. Claiborne, requesting military aid because of fears of a slave revolt.
Territorial Papers of the US - volume: 9 page: 327
Judas, Orleans Territory, New Orleans
Judas, Male Partner of Touro

Recommendation, 1 Sept 1804, of William Brown as Collector by the subscribers, merchants, traders, and others of New Orleans
Territorial Papers of the US - volume: 9 page: 290
Karmouch, Narsise, Orleans Territory
Karmouch, Narsise, Male
Petition, 9 Nov 1804, by inhabitants of Pointe Coupee to Gov. Claiborne, requesting military aid because of fears of a slave revolt.
Territorial Papers of the US - volume: 9 page: 327
Kennedy, Orleans Territory, New Orleans
Kennedy, Male Partner with child
Recommendation, 1 Sept 1804, of William Brown as Collector by the subscribers, merchants, traders, and others of New Orleans
Territorial Papers of the US - volume: 9 page: 290
Kenner, Orleans Territory, New Orleans
Kenner, Male **Job:** Merchant
Business partner with Henderson
Memorial to Congress from merchants of New Orleans, 9 Jan 1804, offering allegiance to the US
Territorial Papers of the US - volume: 9 page: 158
Kenner, Orleans Territory, New Orleans
Kenner, Male Partner of Henderson
Recommendation, 1 Sept 1804, of William Brown as Collector by the subscribers, merchants, traders, and others of New Orleans
Territorial Papers of the US - volume: 9 page: 290
Kenner, William, Orleans Territory, New Orleans
Kenner, William, Male **Job:** Merchant "possessing Considerable property in the City"
Persons recommended by Governor Claiborne for members of the Legislative Council of the Orleans Territory, 17 August 1804.
Territorial Papers of the US - volume: 9 page: 277
Kerr, Lewis, Orleans Territory, New Orleans
Kerr, Lewis, Male **Job:** Sheriff
Lawyer, from Ohio, late of Natchez
Letter, 30 Aug 1804, from Governor Claiborne to the President
Territorial Papers of the US - volume: 9 page: 286
Kerr, Ls, Orleans Territory, New Orleans
Kerr, Ls, Male
Recommendation, 1 Sept 1804, of William Brown as Collector by the subscribers, merchants, traders, and others of New Orleans
Territorial Papers of the US - volume: 9 page: 290

La Chiapella, Geromo,   Orleans Territory, New Orleans
          La Chiapella, Geromo,   Male
Recommendation, 1 Sept 1804, of William Brown as Collector by the subscribers, merchants, traders, and others of New Orleans
Territorial Papers of the US - volume: 9 page: 290
Labattus,   Orleans Territory, New Orleans
          Labattus,   Male
Characterization of New Orleans residents, 1 July 1804
Territorial Papers of the US - volume: 9 page: 250
Labattus,   Orleans Territory, New Orleans
          Labattus,   Male   **Job:**   Merchant
Characterization of New Orleans residents, 1 July 1804
Territorial Papers of the US - volume: 9 page: 252
Labatut,   Orleans Territory, New Orleans
          Labatut,   Male
Recommendation, 1 Sept 1804, of William Brown as Collector by the subscribers, merchants, traders, and others of New Orleans
Territorial Papers of the US - volume: 9 page: 290
Labatut,   Orleans Territory, New Orleans
          Labatut,   Male
Petition, 17 Sep 1804, by inhabitants & colonists of LA to Gov. Claiborne, requesting a commission be established for fear of a slave revolt.
Territorial Papers of the US - volume: 9 page: 296
Labatut,   Orleans Territory, New Orleans
          Labatut,   Male   **Job:**   Merchant
Memorial to Congress from merchants of New Orleans, 9 Jan 1804, offering allegiance to the US
Territorial Papers of the US - volume: 9 page: 158
Labe, Juan,   Orleans Territory
          Labe, Juan,   Male
Petition, 9 Nov 1804, by inhabitants of Pointe Coupee to Gov. Claiborne, requesting military aid because of fears of a slave revolt.
Territorial Papers of the US - volume: 9 page: 327
Labigarre,   Orleans Territory, New Orleans
          Labigarre,   Male   **Born   in:**
          France "married a Livingston, sells Antiseptic gas"
Characterization of New Orleans residents, 1 July 1804
Territorial Papers of the US - volume: 9 page: 258
Labigarre,   Orleans Territory, New Orleans
          Labigarre,   Male

Characterization of New Orleans residents, 1 July 1804
Territorial Papers of the US - volume: 9 page: 257
Lackwood, Saml,   Orleans Territory, New Orleans
          Lackwood, Saml,   Male
Recommendation, 1 Sept 1804, of William Brown as Collector by the subscribers, merchants, traders, and others of New Orleans
Territorial Papers of the US - volume: 9 page: 290
Lacours, Ve,   Orleans Territory
          Lacours, Ve,   Male
Petition, 9 Nov 1804, by inhabitants of Pointe Coupee to Gov. Claiborne, requesting military aid because of fears of a slave revolt.
Territorial Papers of the US - volume: 9 page: 326
Langlois, Baptiste,   Orleans Territory
          Langlois, Baptiste,   Male
Petition, 9 Nov 1804, by inhabitants of Pointe Coupee to Gov. Claiborne, requesting military aid because of fears of a slave revolt.
Territorial Papers of the US - volume: 9 page: 327
Langlois, Louis,   Orleans Territory
          Langlois, Louis,   Male
Petition, 9 Nov 1804, by inhabitants of Pointe Coupee to Gov. Claiborne, requesting military aid because of fears of a slave revolt.
Territorial Papers of the US - volume: 9 page: 327
Lanthis,   Orleans Territory, New Orleans
          Lanthis,   Male
Characterization of New Orleans residents, 1 July 1804
Territorial Papers of the US - volume: 9 page: 250
Lanthoir, John,   Orleans Territory, New Orleans
          Lanthoir, John, Male
Recommendation, 1 Sept 1804, of William Brown as Collector by the subscribers, merchants, traders, and others of New Orleans
Territorial Papers of the US - volume: 9 page: 290
Lanthois,   Orleans Territory, New Orleans
          Lanthois,   Male   **Job:**   Merchant
          Business partner of Pitot
Memorial to Congress from merchants of New Orleans, 9 Jan 1804, offering allegiance to the US
Territorial Papers of the US - volume: 9 page: 158
Lanthois,   Orleans Territory, New Orleans
          Lanthois,   Male   **Job:**   Merchant
          "partner of Mr Pitot"

Characterization of New Orleans residents, 1 July 1804
Territorial Papers of the US - volume: 9 page: 252
Lanusse, Orleans Territory, New Orleans
Lanusse, Male **Job:** Businessman
Characterization of New Orleans residents, 1 July 1804
Territorial Papers of the US - volume: 9 page: 249
Lanusse, Paul, Orleans Territory, New Orleans
Lanusse, Paul, Male
Recommendation, 1 Sept 1804, of William Brown as Collector by the subscribers, merchants, traders, and others of New Orleans
Territorial Papers of the US - volume: 9 page: 290
Lanusse, Paul, Orleans Territory, New Orleans
Lanusse, Paul, Male **Job:** Merchant
Memorial to Congress from merchants of New Orleans, 9 Jan 1804, offering allegiance to the US
Territorial Papers of the US - volume: 9 page: 158
Lanusse, Paul, Orleans Territory, New Orleans
Lanusse, Paul, Male **Job:** Merchant
Characterization of New Orleans residents, 1 July 1804
Territorial Papers of the US - volume: 9 page: 252
Lauran, Pre, Orleans Territory
Lauran, Pre, Male
Petition, 9 Nov 1804, by inhabitants of Pointe Coupee to Gov. Claiborne, requesting military aid because of fears of a slave revolt.
Territorial Papers of the US - volume: 9 page: 327
Laussat, Orleans Territory, New Orleans
Laussat, Male **Job:** Prefect
Characterization of New Orleans residents, 1 July 1804
Territorial Papers of the US - volume: 9 page: 253
Laussat, Orleans Territory, New Orleans
Laussat, Male **Job:** Prefect
Characterization of New Orleans residents, 1 July 1804
Territorial Papers of the US - volume: 9 page: 252
Lavandois, Senr Orleans Territory, New Orleans
Lavandois, SenrMale "one of oldest Creoles, illiterate and ignorant, immense fortune"
Characterization of New Orleans residents, 1 July 1804
Territorial Papers of the US - volume: 9 page: 255
Le Dut, V., Orleans Territory
Le Dut, V., Male **Color:** Colored
Address from the free people of color Jan. 1804, volunteering for military service
Territorial Papers of the US - volume: 9 page: 174
LeBeau, Fcols, Orleans Territory
LeBeau, Fcols, Male
Petition, 9 Nov 1804, by inhabitants of Pointe Coupee to Gov. Claiborne, requesting military aid because of fears of a slave revolt.
Territorial Papers of the US - volume: 9 page: 327
LeBlanc, Are, Orleans Territory
LeBlanc, Are, Male
Petition, 9 Nov 1804, by inhabitants of Pointe Coupee to Gov. Claiborne, requesting military aid because of fears of a slave revolt.
Territorial Papers of the US - volume: 9 page: 327
LeDoux, Orleans Territory
LeDoux, Male
Petition, 9 Nov 1804, by inhabitants of Pointe Coupee to Gov. Claiborne, requesting military aid because of fears of a slave revolt.
Territorial Papers of the US - volume: 9 page: 327
Ledoux, Joseph, Orleans Territory
Ledoux, Joseph, Male
Petition, 9 Nov 1804, by inhabitants of Pointe Coupee to Gov. Claiborne, requesting military aid because of fears of a slave revolt.
Territorial Papers of the US - volume: 9 page: 327
Ledoux, Valn, Orleans Territory
Ledoux, Valn, Male
Petition, 9 Nov 1804, by inhabitants of Pointe Coupee to Gov. Claiborne, requesting military aid because of fears of a slave revolt.
Territorial Papers of the US - volume: 9 page: 327
Ledoux, Vn, Orleans Territory
Ledoux, Vn, Male
Petition, 9 Nov 1804, by inhabitants of Pointe Coupee to Gov. Claiborne, requesting military aid because of fears of a slave revolt.
Territorial Papers of the US - volume: 9 page: 326
Lejeune, Charles, Orleans Territory
Lejeune, Charles, Male
Petition, 9 Nov 1804, by inhabitants of Pointe Coupee to Gov. Claiborne, requesting military aid because of fears of a slave revolt.
Territorial Papers of the US - volume: 9 page: 327
Lejeune, Michelle, Orleans Territory
Lejeune, Michelle, Male
Petition, 9 Nov 1804, by inhabitants of Pointe Coupee to Gov. Claiborne, requesting military aid because of fears of a slave revolt.

Territorial Papers of the US - volume: 9 page: 327
Levandois, Junr   Orleans Territory, New Orleans
        Levandois, Junr Male   **Job:**   Planter
Characterization of New Orleans residents, 1 July 1804
Territorial Papers of the US - volume: 9 page: 253
Liotant, Louis,   Orleans Territory
        Liotant, Louis, Male   **Color:** Colored
Address from the free people of color Jan. 1804, volunteering for military service
Territorial Papers of the US - volume: 9 page: 175
Livandois, junr   Orleans Territory, New Orleans
        Livandois, junr Male
Characterization of New Orleans residents, 1 July 1804
Territorial Papers of the US - volume: 9 page: 250
Livandois, Senr   Orleans Territory, New Orleans
        Livandois, Senr Male   **Job:**   Planter
Characterization of New Orleans residents, 1 July 1804
Territorial Papers of the US - volume: 9 page: 253
Livandois, Sr Orleans Territory, New Orleans
        Livandois, Sr Male   "wealthy"
Characterization of New Orleans residents, 1 July 1804
Territorial Papers of the US - volume: 9 page: 250
Livingston, Edw,   Orleans Territory, New Orleans
        Livingston, Edw,   Male
Recommendation, 1 Sept 1804, of William Brown as Collector by the subscribers, merchants, traders, and others of New Orleans
Territorial Papers of the US - volume: 9 page: 290
Loviell, Messr Orleans Territory, Attakapas
        Loviell, Messr Male   **Job:**   "French Planter"
Persons recommended by Governor Claiborne for members of the Legislative Council of the Orleans Territory, 17 August 1804.
Territorial Papers of the US - volume: 9 page: 278
Madan, P,   Orleans Territory, New Orleans
        Madan, P,   Male   & Co.
Recommendation, 1 Sept 1804, of William Brown as Collector by the subscribers, merchants, traders, and others of New Orleans
Territorial Papers of the US - volume: 9 page: 290
Maidesingue, Baptiste,   Orleans Territory

        Maidesingue, Baptiste, Male   **Color:** Colored
Address from the free people of color Jan. 1804, volunteering for military service
Territorial Papers of the US - volume: 9 page: 175
Major, Orleans Territory
        Major, Male
Petition, 9 Nov 1804, by inhabitants of Pointe Coupee to Gov. Claiborne, requesting military aid because of fears of a slave revolt.
Territorial Papers of the US - volume: 9 page: 327
Major, Pierre, Orleans Territory
        Major, Pierre, Male
Petition, 9 Nov 1804, by inhabitants of Pointe Coupee to Gov. Claiborne, requesting military aid because of fears of a slave revolt.
Territorial Papers of the US - volume: 9 page: 327
Marange, Senr Orleans Territory, New Orleans
        Marange,   Male **Job:**   Planter
        "has been Clerk of the Court"
Characterization of New Orleans residents, 1 July 1804
Territorial Papers of the US - volume: 9 page: 251
Marigny,   Orleans Territory, New Orleans
        Marigny,   Male
Characterization of New Orleans residents, 1 July 1804
Territorial Papers of the US - volume: 9 page: 254
Martinez, M., Orleans Territory, New Orleans
        Martinez, M., Male   **Job:**   Merchant
Memorial to Congress from merchants of New Orleans, 9 Jan 1804, offering allegiance to the US
Territorial Papers of the US - volume: 9 page: 158
Matata, Celestin,   Orleans Territory
        Matata, Celestin,   Male   **Color:** Colored
Address from the free people of color Jan. 1804, volunteering for military service
Territorial Papers of the US - volume: 9 page: 175
Mather,   Orleans Territory, New Orleans
        Mather,   Male   **Job:**   Planter
Characterization of New Orleans residents, 1 July 1804
Territorial Papers of the US - volume: 9 page: 251
Mather, James,   Orleans   Territory, Between Manshac & New Orleans
        Mather, James, Male   "a   native   of England who has resided in this country a number of years on a valuable plantation."

Persons recommended by Governor Claiborne for members of the Legislative Council of the Orleans Territory, 17 August 1804.
Territorial Papers of the US - volume: 9 page: 277
Mayeux,   Orleans Territory
        Mayeux,   Male
Petition, 9 Nov 1804, by inhabitants of Pointe Coupee to Gov. Claiborne, requesting military aid because of fears of a slave revolt.
Territorial Papers of the US - volume: 9 page: 326
McDonogh, John, Junr   Orleans Territory, New Orleans
        McDonogh, John, Jr.   Male   **Job:** Merchant
Memorial to Congress from merchants of New Orleans, 9 Jan 1804, offering allegiance to the US
Territorial Papers of the US - volume: 9 page: 158
McNeal,   Orleans Territory, New Orleans
        McNeal,   Male   Partner   of Montgomery
Recommendation, 1 Sept 1804, of William Brown as Collector by the subscribers, merchants, traders, and others of New Orleans
Territorial Papers of the US - volume: 9 page: 290
McNeal,   Orleans Territory, New Orleans
        McNeal,   Male   **Job:** Merchant
        Business partner of Montgomery
Memorial to Congress from merchants of New Orleans, 9 Jan 1804, offering allegiance to the US
Territorial Papers of the US - volume: 9 page: 158
Mdonogh, John, Jr   Orleans Territory, New Orleans
        Mdonogh, John, Jr   Male   & Co.
Recommendation, 1 Sept 1804, of William Brown as Collector by the subscribers, merchants, traders, and others of New Orleans
Territorial Papers of the US - volume: 9 page: 290
Meeker,   Orleans Territory, New Orleans
        Meeker,   Male   **Job:** Merchant
        Business partner of Williamson & Patton
Memorial to Congress from merchants of New Orleans, 9 Jan 1804, offering allegiance to the US
Territorial Papers of the US - volume: 9 page: 158
Meeker,   Orleans Territory, New Orleans
        Meeker,   Male   Partner   of Williamson & Patton
Recommendation, 1 Sept 1804, of William Brown as Collector by the subscribers, merchants, traders, and others of New Orleans
Territorial Papers of the US - volume: 9 page: 290

Merieult, Jn Frs,   Orleans Territory, New Orleans
        Merieult, Jn Frs,   Male
Petition, 17 Sep 1804, by inhabitants & colonists of LA to Gov. Claiborne, requesting a commission be established for fear of a slave revolt.
Territorial Papers of the US - volume: 9 page: 296
Merieult, John F.,   Orleans Territory, New Orleans
        Merieult, John F.,   Male   **Job:** Merchant
Memorial to Congress from merchants of New Orleans, 9 Jan 1804, offering allegiance to the US
Territorial Papers of the US - volume: 9 page: 158
Merieult, John F.,   Orleans Territory, New Orleans
        Merieult, John F.,   Male
Recommendation, 1 Sept 1804, of William Brown as Collector by the subscribers, merchants, traders, and others of New Orleans
Territorial Papers of the US - volume: 9 page: 290
Merieure, Jean,   Orleans Territory, New Orleans
        Merieure, Jean, Male   **Job:** Merchant
Characterization of New Orleans residents, 1 July 1804
Territorial Papers of the US - volume: 9 page: 251
Merieux,   Orleans Territory, New Orleans
        Merieux,   Male   **Born   in:** France "not a Merchant supposed to be rich"
Characterization of New Orleans residents, 1 July 1804
Territorial Papers of the US - volume: 9 page: 249
Merme, S.,   Orleans Territory, New Orleans
        Merme, S.,   Male   **Job:** Merchant
Memorial to Congress from merchants of New Orleans, 9 Jan 1804, offering allegiance to the US
Territorial Papers of the US - volume: 9 page: 158
Meyange,   Orleans Territory, New Orleans
        Meyange,   Male   **Born   in:** France
Characterization of New Orleans residents, 1 July 1804
Territorial Papers of the US - volume: 9 page: 249
Milne, Alexr, Orleans Territory, New Orleans
        Milne, Alexr,   Male   **Job:** Merchant
Memorial to Congress from merchants of New Orleans, 9 Jan 1804, offering allegiance to the US
Territorial Papers of the US - volume: 9 page: 158

Molier, H.,　　Orleans Territory, New Orleans
　　　　Molier, H.,　　Male　& Company
Recommendation, 1 Sept 1804, of William Brown
as Collector by the subscribers, merchants, traders,
and others of New Orleans
Territorial Papers of the US - volume: 9 page: 290
Molier, Henry,　　　Orleans Territory, New
Orleans
　　　　Molier, Henry, Male　**Job:**　Merchant
Memorial to Congress from merchants of New
Orleans, 9 Jan 1804, offering allegiance to the US
Territorial Papers of the US - volume: 9 page: 158
Montague,　Orleans Territory, New Orleans
　　　　Montague,　　Male　**Job:**　Doctor
　　　　"advanced in years who has grown with
the City of New Orleans"
Characterization of New Orleans residents, 1 July
1804
Territorial Papers of the US - volume: 9 page: 255
Montgomery, Orleans Territory, New Orleans
　　　　Montgomery, Male　**Job:**　Merchant
　　　　Business partner of McNeal
Memorial to Congress from merchants of New
Orleans, 9 Jan 1804, offering allegiance to the US
Territorial Papers of the US - volume: 9 page: 158
Montgomery, Orleans Territory, New Orleans
　　　　Montgomery,　　Male　Partner of McNeal
Recommendation, 1 Sept 1804, of William Brown
as Collector by the subscribers, merchants, traders,
and others of New Orleans
Territorial Papers of the US - volume: 9 page: 290
Morgan,　　Orleans Territory, New Orleans
　　　　Morgan,　　　Male　Partner of Pollock
Recommendation, 1 Sept 1804, of William Brown
as Collector by the subscribers, merchants, traders,
and others of New Orleans
Territorial Papers of the US - volume: 9 page: 290
Morgan,　　Orleans Territory, New Orleans
　　　　Morgan,　　　Male　**Job:**　Merchant
Characterization of New Orleans residents, 1 July
1804
Territorial Papers of the US - volume: 9 page: 251
Morgan, B.,　Orleans Territory, New Orleans
　　　　Morgan, B.,　　Male
Characterization of New Orleans residents, 1 July
1804
Territorial Papers of the US - volume: 9 page: 256
Morgan, Benja,　　　Orleans Territory, New
Orleans
　　　　Morgan, Benja, Male

Recommendation, 1 Sept 1804, of William Brown
as Collector by the subscribers, merchants, traders,
and others of New Orleans
Territorial Papers of the US - volume: 9 page: 290
Morgan, Benjamim,　Orleans Territory, New
Orleans
　　　　Morgan, Benjamim,　Male
Persons recommended by Governor Claiborne for
members of the Legislative Council of the Orleans
Territory, 17 August 1804.
Territorial Papers of the US - volume: 9 page: 277
Morgan, George W.,　Orleans Territory, New
Orleans
　　　　Morgan, George W.,　Male
Recommendation, 1 Sept 1804, of William Brown
as Collector by the subscribers, merchants, traders,
and others of New Orleans
Territorial Papers of the US - volume: 9 page: 290
Mumford,　Orleans Territory, New Orleans
　　　　Mumford,　　Male　Partner of Gelston
Recommendation, 1 Sept 1804, of William Brown
as Collector by the subscribers, merchants, traders,
and others of New Orleans
Territorial Papers of the US - volume: 9 page: 290
Nichols, Ed,　Orleans Territory, New Orleans
　　　　Nichols, Ed,　　Male　**Job:**　Clerk　of
the Court　　　Lawyer, late of Maryland
Letter, 30 Aug 1804, from Governor Claiborne to
the President
Territorial Papers of the US - volume: 9 page: 286
Nique, George,　　　Orleans Territory
　　　　Nique, George, Male
Petition, 9 Nov 1804, by inhabitants of Pointe
Coupee to Gov. Claiborne, requesting military aid
because of fears of a slave revolt.
Territorial Papers of the US - volume: 9 page: 327
O'Hara, H.,　Orleans Territory, New Orleans
　　　　O'Hara, H.,　　Male　Partner　of　J.B.
Farrell
Recommendation, 1 Sept 1804, of William Brown
as Collector by the subscribers, merchants, traders,
and others of New Orleans
Territorial Papers of the US - volume: 9 page: 290
O'Hara, H.,　Orleans Territory, New Orleans
　　　　O'Hara, H.,　　Male　**Job:**　Merchant
　　　　Business partner of J.B. Farrell
Memorial to Congress from merchants of New
Orleans, 9 Jan 1804, offering allegiance to the US
Territorial Papers of the US - volume: 9 page: 158
Olainde, Bapthmle,　　Orleans Territory

Olainde, Bapthmle,   Male
Petition, 9 Nov 1804, by inhabitants of Pointe Coupee to Gov. Claiborne, requesting military aid because of fears of a slave revolt.
Territorial Papers of the US - volume: 9 page: 327
Olainde, Pelice,   Orleans Territory
Olainde, Pelice,   Male
Petition, 9 Nov 1804, by inhabitants of Pointe Coupee to Gov. Claiborne, requesting military aid because of fears of a slave revolt.
Territorial Papers of the US - volume: 9 page: 327
Orgenois, Breton,   Orleans Territory, New Orleans
Orgenois, Breton,   Male   "rich planter"
Characterization of New Orleans residents, 1 July 1804
Territorial Papers of the US - volume: 9 page: 250
Orgenois, De Breton, Orleans Territory, New Orleans
Orgenois, De Breton,   Male   **Job:** Planter
Characterization of New Orleans residents, 1 July 1804
Territorial Papers of the US - volume: 9 page: 253
Palfrey, Jno, Jr   Orleans Territory, New Orleans
Palfrey, Jno, Jr Male
Recommendation, 1 Sept 1804, of William Brown as Collector by the subscribers, merchants, traders, and others of New Orleans
Territorial Papers of the US - volume: 9 page: 290
Pamias, Salvador,   Orleans Territory
Pamias, Salvador,   Male
Petition, 9 Nov 1804, by inhabitants of Pointe Coupee to Gov. Claiborne, requesting military aid because of fears of a slave revolt.
Territorial Papers of the US - volume: 9 page: 327
Passement, Jn Bte,   Orleans Territory, New Orleans
Passement, Jn Bte,   Male   **Job:** Merchant
Memorial to Congress from merchants of New Orleans, 9 Jan 1804, offering allegiance to the US
Territorial Papers of the US - volume: 9 page: 158
Patin, Antoine,   Orleans Territory
Patin, Antoine, Male
Petition, 9 Nov 1804, by inhabitants of Pointe Coupee to Gov. Claiborne, requesting military aid because of fears of a slave revolt.
Territorial Papers of the US - volume: 9 page: 327
Patin, Joseph, Orleans Territory
Patin, Joseph,   Male
Petition, 9 Nov 1804, by inhabitants of Pointe Coupee to Gov. Claiborne, requesting military aid because of fears of a slave revolt.
Territorial Papers of the US - volume: 9 page: 327
Patin, Veuve, Orleans Territory
Patin, Veuve,   Male
Petition, 9 Nov 1804, by inhabitants of Pointe Coupee to Gov. Claiborne, requesting military aid because of fears of a slave revolt.
Territorial Papers of the US - volume: 9 page: 327
Patton,   Orleans Territory, New Orleans
Patton, Male   Partner of Meeker & Williamson
Recommendation, 1 Sept 1804, of William Brown as Collector by the subscribers, merchants, traders, and others of New Orleans
Territorial Papers of the US - volume: 9 page: 290
Patton,   Orleans Territory, New Orleans
Patton, Male   **Job:** Merchant
Business partner of Meeker & Williamson
Memorial to Congress from merchants of New Orleans, 9 Jan 1804, offering allegiance to the US
Territorial Papers of the US - volume: 9 page: 158
Payfare,   Orleans Territory, New Orleans
Payfare,   Male
Characterization of New Orleans residents, 1 July 1804
Territorial Papers of the US - volume: 9 page: 249
Paysarey,   Orleans Territory, New Orleans
Paysarey,   Male
Characterization of New Orleans residents, 1 July 1804
Territorial Papers of the US - volume: 9 page: 249
Paysarey,   Orleans Territory, New Orleans
Paysarey,   Male   **Job:** Retired Merchant
Characterization of New Orleans residents, 1 July 1804
Territorial Papers of the US - volume: 9 page: 252
Perot, Pierre, Orleans Territory
Perot, Pierre,   Male
Petition, 9 Nov 1804, by inhabitants of Pointe Coupee to Gov. Claiborne, requesting military aid because of fears of a slave revolt.
Territorial Papers of the US - volume: 9 page: 327
Petit,   Orleans Territory, New Orleans
Petit,   Male

Characterization of New Orleans residents, 1 July 1804
Territorial Papers of the US - volume: 9 page: 256
Petit,   Orleans Territory, New Orleans
      Petit,   Male   **Job:**   Businessman
Characterization of New Orleans residents, 1 July 1804
Territorial Papers of the US - volume: 9 page: 249
Petit,   Orleans Territory, New Orleans
      Petit,   Male   **Job:**   Merchant
      Born in: England
Characterization of New Orleans residents, 1 July 1804
Territorial Papers of the US - volume: 9 page: 252
Petit, Peter,   Orleans Territory, New Orleans
      Petit, Peter,   Male   **Job:**   Merchant
Persons recommended by Governor Claiborne for members of the Legislative Council of the Orleans Territory, 17 August 1804.
Territorial Papers of the US - volume: 9 page: 277
Petit, Pre,   Orleans Territory, New Orleans
      Petit, Pre,   Male   **Job:**   Merchant
Memorial to Congress from merchants of New Orleans, 9 Jan 1804, offering allegiance to the US
Territorial Papers of the US - volume: 9 page: 158
Petits, Orleans Territory, New Orleans
      Petits,   Male
Characterization of New Orleans residents, 1 July 1804
Territorial Papers of the US - volume: 9 page: 254
Peytavin,   Orleans Territory, New Orleans
      Peytavin,   Male
Petition, 17 Sep 1804, by inhabitants & colonists of LA to Gov. Claiborne, requesting a commission be established for fear of a slave revolt.
Territorial Papers of the US - volume: 9 page: 296
Peytavin,   Orleans Territory, New Orleans
      Peytavin,   Male   **Job:**   Merchant
      Business partner of Reynaud
Memorial to Congress from merchants of New Orleans, 9 Jan 1804, offering allegiance to the US
Territorial Papers of the US - volume: 9 page: 158
Peytavin,   Orleans Territory, New Orleans
      Peytavin,   Male   Partner   of Reynaud
Recommendation, 1 Sept 1804, of William Brown as Collector by the subscribers, merchants, traders, and others of New Orleans
Territorial Papers of the US - volume: 9 page: 290
Philippon, Jr   Orleans Territory, New Orleans
      Philippon, Jr   Male
Recommendation, 1 Sept 1804, of William Brown as Collector by the subscribers, merchants, traders, and others of New Orleans
Territorial Papers of the US - volume: 9 page: 290
Philippon, Fs,   Orleans Territory, New Orleans
      Philippon, Fs,   Male   **Job:**   Merchant
Memorial to Congress from merchants of New Orleans, 9 Jan 1804, offering allegiance to the US
Territorial Papers of the US - volume: 9 page: 158
Pierre, Baptiste,   Orleans Territory
      Pierre, Baptiste,   Male   **Color:**   Colored
Address from the free people of color Jan. 1804, volunteering for military service
Territorial Papers of the US - volume: 9 page: 175
Pitot,   Orleans Territory, New Orleans
      Pitot,   Male
Characterization of New Orleans residents, 1 July 1804
Territorial Papers of the US - volume: 9 page: 256
Pitot,   Orleans Territory, New Orleans
      Pitot,   Male   **Job:**   Merchant
Characterization of New Orleans residents, 1 July 1804
Territorial Papers of the US - volume: 9 page: 252
Pitot,   Orleans Territory, New Orleans
      Pitot,   Male   **Job:**   Merchant
      Business partner of Lanthois
Memorial to Congress from merchants of New Orleans, 9 Jan 1804, offering allegiance to the US
Territorial Papers of the US - volume: 9 page: 158
Pitot,   Orleans Territory, New Orleans
      Pitot,   Male
Characterization of New Orleans residents, 1 July 1804
Territorial Papers of the US - volume: 9 page: 250
Pitot, James,   Orleans Territory, New Orleans
      Pitot, James,   Male   **Job:**   Merchant
      "French" . Received from the Gov. the "appointment of Mayor on the recommendation of the Municipality"
Persons recommended by Governor Claiborne for members of the Legislative Council of the Orleans Territory, 17 August 1804.
Territorial Papers of the US - volume: 9 page: 277
Pitot, Js,   Orleans Territory, New Orleans
      Pitot, Js,   Male   **Job:**   Mayor
Recommendation, 1 Sept 1804, of William Brown

as Collector by the subscribers, merchants, traders, and others of New Orleans
Territorial Papers of the US - volume: 9 page: 290
Pitot, Js,   Orleans Territory, New Orleans
Pitot, Js,   Male
Petition, 17 Sep 1804, by inhabitants & colonists of LA to Gov. Claiborne, requesting a commission be established for fear of a slave revolt.
Territorial Papers of the US - volume: 9 page: 296
Planche, Ander,   Orleans Territory
Planche, Ander,   Male
Petition, 9 Nov 1804, by inhabitants of Pointe Coupee to Gov. Claiborne, requesting military aid because of fears of a slave revolt.
Territorial Papers of the US - volume: 9 page: 326
Poche, Josephe,   Orleans Territory
Poche, Josephe,   Male
Petition, 9 Nov 1804, by inhabitants of Pointe Coupee to Gov. Claiborne, requesting military aid because of fears of a slave revolt.
Territorial Papers of the US - volume: 9 page: 327
Pollock,   Orleans Territory, New Orleans
Pollock,   Male   Partner of Morgan
Recommendation, 1 Sept 1804, of William Brown as Collector by the subscribers, merchants, traders, and others of New Orleans
Territorial Papers of the US - volume: 9 page: 290
Pollock, George,   Orleans Territory, New Orleans
Pollock, George,   Male   **Job:** merchant   "an Irishman, but long in New York", educated, citizen of New Orleans
Characterization of New Orleans residents, 1 July 1804
Territorial Papers of the US - volume: 9 page: 256
Pollock, George,   Orleans Territory, New Orleans
Pollock, George,   Male
Recommendation, 1 Sept 1804, of William Brown as Collector by the subscribers, merchants, traders, and others of New Orleans
Territorial Papers of the US - volume: 9 page: 290
Pollock, George,   Orleans Territory, New Orleans
Pollock, George,   Male   **Job:** Merchant
Memorial to Congress from merchants of New Orleans, 9 Jan 1804, offering allegiance to the US
Territorial Papers of the US - volume: 9 page: 158
Pomet, Leonard,   Orleans Territory

Pomet, Leonard,   Male   **Color:** Colored
Address from the free people of color Jan. 1804, volunteering for military service
Territorial Papers of the US - volume: 9 page: 174
Ponnas, L.,   Orleans Territory, New Orleans
Ponnas, L.,   Male
Recommendation, 1 Sept 1804, of William Brown as Collector by the subscribers, merchants, traders, and others of New Orleans
Territorial Papers of the US - volume: 9 page: 290
Populos, Maurice,   Orleans Territory
Populos, Maurice,   Male   **Color:** Colored
Address from the free people of color Jan. 1804, volunteering for military service
Territorial Papers of the US - volume: 9 page: 175
Populus, Celestin,   Orleans Territory
Populus, Celestin,   Male   **Color:** Colored
Address from the free people of color Jan. 1804, volunteering for military service
Territorial Papers of the US - volume: 9 page: 175
Populuse, Entoine,   Orleans Territory
Populuse, Entoine,   Male   **Color:** Colored
Address from the free people of color Jan. 1804, volunteering for military service
Territorial Papers of the US - volume: 9 page: 174
Poque or Boque, George,   Orleans Territory
Poque or Boque, George,   Male
Petition, 9 Nov 1804, by inhabitants of Pointe Coupee to Gov. Claiborne, requesting military aid because of fears of a slave revolt.
Territorial Papers of the US - volume: 9 page: 327
Porche, J. Baptiste,   Orleans Territory
Porche, J. Baptiste,   Male
Petition, 9 Nov 1804, by inhabitants of Pointe Coupee to Gov. Claiborne, requesting military aid because of fears of a slave revolt.
Territorial Papers of the US - volume: 9 page: 327
Porche, Michelle,   Orleans Territory
Porche, Michelle,   Male
Petition, 9 Nov 1804, by inhabitants of Pointe Coupee to Gov. Claiborne, requesting military aid because of fears of a slave revolt.
Territorial Papers of the US - volume: 9 page: 327
Porche, Simon,   Orleans Territory
Porche, Simon, Male

Petition, 9 Nov 1804, by inhabitants of Pointe Coupee to Gov. Claiborne, requesting military aid because of fears of a slave revolt.
Territorial Papers of the US - volume: 9 page: 327
Porches, Francois,   Orleans Territory
        Porches, Francois,   Male
Petition, 9 Nov 1804, by inhabitants of Pointe Coupee to Gov. Claiborne, requesting military aid because of fears of a slave revolt.
Territorial Papers of the US - volume: 9 page: 327
Poree, Orleans Territory, New Orleans
        Poree, Male
Characterization of New Orleans residents, 1 July 1804
Territorial Papers of the US - volume: 9 page: 250
Poree, Charles,   Orleans Territory
        Poree, Charles, Male   **Color:** Colored
Address from the free people of color Jan. 1804, volunteering for military service
Territorial Papers of the US - volume: 9 page: 175
Poree, Chas,   Orleans Territory, New Orleans
        Poree, Chas,   Male
Petition, 17 Sep 1804, by inhabitants & colonists of LA to Gov. Claiborne, requesting a commission be established for fear of a slave revolt.
Territorial Papers of the US - volume: 9 page: 296
Poree, Thomas,   Orleans Territory, New Orleans
        Poree, Thomas, Male   **Job:** Planter
Characterization of New Orleans residents, 1 July 1804
Territorial Papers of the US - volume: 9 page: 253
Poree, Voltaire,   Orleans Territory
        Poree, Voltaire,   Male   **Color:** Colored
Address from the free people of color Jan. 1804, volunteering for military service
Territorial Papers of the US - volume: 9 page: 175
Potard,   Orleans Territory
        Potard, Male
Petition, 9 Nov 1804, by inhabitants of Pointe Coupee to Gov. Claiborne, requesting military aid because of fears of a slave revolt.
Territorial Papers of the US - volume: 9 page: 327
Poultney, John, Jr   Orleans Territory, New Orleans
        Poultney, John, Jr   Male   & Co.
Recommendation, 1 Sept 1804, of William Brown as Collector by the subscribers, merchants, traders, and others of New Orleans

Territorial Papers of the US - volume: 9 page: 290
Poultney, John Jr,   Orleans Territory, New Orleans
        Poultney, John Jr,   Male   **Job:** Merchant
Memorial to Congress from merchants of New Orleans, 9 Jan 1804, offering allegiance to the US
Territorial Papers of the US - volume: 9 page: 158
Poursio, George,   Orleans Territory
        Poursio, George,   Male
Petition, 9 Nov 1804, by inhabitants of Pointe Coupee to Gov. Claiborne, requesting military aid because of fears of a slave revolt.
Territorial Papers of the US - volume: 9 page: 327
Poydras,   Orleans Territory, New Orleans
        Poydras,   Male   "of   Pointe Coupee, immense fortune"
Characterization of New Orleans residents, 1 July 1804
Territorial Papers of the US - volume: 9 page: 254
Poydrass, Julian,   Orleans Territory, Pointe Coupee
        Poydrass, Julian,   Male
Persons recommended by Governor Claiborne for members of the Legislative Council of the Orleans Territory, 17 August 1804.
Territorial Papers of the US - volume: 9 page: 277
Prevost,   Orleans Territory, New Orleans
        Prevost,   Male   "Evan   Jones married his sister"
Characterization of New Orleans residents, 1 July 1804
Territorial Papers of the US - volume: 9 page: 255
Prevost,   Orleans Territory, New Orleans
        Prevost,   Male   **Job:** Planter
        "formerly   employed   by   Spanish government"
Characterization of New Orleans residents, 1 July 1804
Territorial Papers of the US - volume: 9 page: 253
Priestly, W,   Orleans Territory
        Priestly, W,   Male
Petition, 9 Nov 1804, by inhabitants of Pointe Coupee to Gov. Claiborne, requesting military aid because of fears of a slave revolt.
Territorial Papers of the US - volume: 9 page: 327
Rand, Ben.,   Orleans Territory
        Rand, Ben.,   Male
Petition, 9 Nov 1804, by inhabitants of Pointe

Coupee to Gov. Claiborne, requesting military aid because of fears of a slave revolt.
Territorial Papers of the US - volume: 9 page: 327
Randall, Thomas, Orleans Territory, New Orleans
Randall, Thomas, Male
Recommendation, 1 Sept 1804, of William Brown as Collector by the subscribers, merchants, traders, and others of New Orleans
Territorial Papers of the US - volume: 9 page: 290
Rayant, Orleans Territory
Rayant, Male
Petition, 9 Nov 1804, by inhabitants of Pointe Coupee to Gov. Claiborne, requesting military aid because of fears of a slave revolt.
Territorial Papers of the US - volume: 9 page: 327
Reaud, A, Orleans Territory, New Orleans
Reaud, A, Male
Recommendation, 1 Sept 1804, of William Brown as Collector by the subscribers, merchants, traders, and others of New Orleans
Territorial Papers of the US - volume: 9 page: 290
Relf, Orleans Territory, New Orleans
Relf, Male Partner of Chew
Recommendation, 1 Sept 1804, of William Brown as Collector by the subscribers, merchants, traders, and others of New Orleans
Territorial Papers of the US - volume: 9 page: 290
Relf, Orleans Territory, New Orleans
Relf, Male **Job:** Merchant
Business partner of Mr. Chew
Memorial to Congress from merchants of New Orleans, 9 Jan 1804, offering allegiance to the US
Territorial Papers of the US - volume: 9 page: 158
Reynaud, Orleans Territory, New Orleans
Reynaud, Male **Job:** Merchant
Business partner of Peytavin
Memorial to Congress from merchants of New Orleans, 9 Jan 1804, offering allegiance to the US
Territorial Papers of the US - volume: 9 page: 158
Reynaud, Orleans Territory, New Orleans
Reynaud, Male Partner of Peytavin
Recommendation, 1 Sept 1804, of William Brown as Collector by the subscribers, merchants, traders, and others of New Orleans
Territorial Papers of the US - volume: 9 page: 290
Reyno, Josef, Orleans Territory, New Orleans
Reyno, Josef, Male **Job:** Merchant

Memorial to Congress from merchants of New Orleans, 9 Jan 1804, offering allegiance to the US
Territorial Papers of the US - volume: 9 page: 158
Robiare, Philippe, Orleans Territory
Robiare, Philippe, Male
Petition, 9 Nov 1804, by inhabitants of Pointe Coupee to Gov. Claiborne, requesting military aid because of fears of a slave revolt.
Territorial Papers of the US - volume: 9 page: 327
Robillard, Pierre, Orleans Territory
Robillard, Pierre, Male
Petition, 9 Nov 1804, by inhabitants of Pointe Coupee to Gov. Claiborne, requesting military aid because of fears of a slave revolt.
Territorial Papers of the US - volume: 9 page: 327
Roman, Orleans Territory, New Orleans
Roman, Male "of the Attackapas . . . of considerable fortune and influence in that settlement"
Characterization of New Orleans residents, 1 July 1804
Territorial Papers of the US - volume: 9 page: 256
Roques, Orleans Territory, New Orleans
Roques, Male
Recommendation, 1 Sept 1804, of William Brown as Collector by the subscribers, merchants, traders, and others of New Orleans
Territorial Papers of the US - volume: 9 page: 290
Roquet?, R., Orleans Territory, New Orleans
Roquet?, R., Male **Job:** Merchant
Memorial to Congress from merchants of New Orleans, 9 Jan 1804, offering allegiance to the US
Territorial Papers of the US - volume: 9 page: 158
Rosemone, Miniere, Orleans Territory
Rosemone, Miniere, Male **Color:** Colored
Address from the free people of color Jan. 1804, volunteering for military service
Territorial Papers of the US - volume: 9 page: 175
Rougaud, Orleans Territory, New Orleans
Rougaud, Male
Petition, 17 Sep 1804, by inhabitants & colonists of LA to Gov. Claiborne, requesting a commission be established for fear of a slave revolt.
Territorial Papers of the US - volume: 9 page: 296
Rousaire, Baptiste, Orleans Territory
Rousaire, Baptiste, Male **Color:** Colored
Address from the free people of color Jan. 1804, volunteering for military service

Territorial Papers of the US - volume: 9 page: 174
Rouzan, Tn Messa, Orleans Territory, New Orleans
Rouzan, Tn Messa, Male Name hard to read
Recommendation, 1 Sept 1804, of William Brown as Collector by the subscribers, merchants, traders, and others of New Orleans
Territorial Papers of the US - volume: 9 page: 290
Rouzon, Tn Messre, Orleans Territory, New Orleans
Rouzon, Tn Messre, Male
Petition, 17 Sep 1804, by inhabitants & colonists of LA to Gov. Claiborne, requesting a commission be established for fear of a slave revolt.
Territorial Papers of the US - volume: 9 page: 296
Saisan "pere", Baptiste, Orleans Territory
Saisan "pere", Baptiste, Male
Petition, 9 Nov 1804, by inhabitants of Pointe Coupee to Gov. Claiborne, requesting military aid because of fears of a slave revolt.
Territorial Papers of the US - volume: 9 page: 327
Samson, Orleans Territory
Samson, Male
Petition, 9 Nov 1804, by inhabitants of Pointe Coupee to Gov. Claiborne, requesting military aid because of fears of a slave revolt.
Territorial Papers of the US - volume: 9 page: 327
Sanderson, John P., Orleans Territory, New Orleans
Sanderson, John P., Male
Recommendation, 1 Sept 1804, of William Brown as Collector by the subscribers, merchants, traders, and others of New Orleans
Territorial Papers of the US - volume: 9 page: 290
Sanderson, John P., Orleans Territory, New Orleans
Sanderson, John P., Male **Job:** Merchant
Memorial to Congress from merchants of New Orleans, 9 Jan 1804, offering allegiance to the US
Territorial Papers of the US - volume: 9 page: 158
Sarrieux, Jemn, Orleans Territory
Sarrieux, Jemn, Male **Color:** Colored
Address from the free people of color Jan. 1804, volunteering for military service
Territorial Papers of the US - volume: 9 page: 175
Sarriey, Ene, Orleans Territory
Sarriey, Ene, Male **Color:** Colored

Address from the free people of color Jan. 1804, volunteering for military service
Territorial Papers of the US - volume: 9 page: 175
Saseier, Jn, Orleans Territory
Saseier, Jn, Male **Color:** Colored
Address from the free people of color Jan. 1804, volunteering for military service
Territorial Papers of the US - volume: 9 page: 174
Saulet, Etienne, Orleans Territory
Saulet, Etienne, Male **Color:** Colored
Address from the free people of color Jan. 1804, volunteering for military service
Territorial Papers of the US - volume: 9 page: 175
Sauve, Orleans Territory, New Orleans
Sauve, Male **Job:** planter **Born in:** France "wealthy"
Characterization of New Orleans residents, 1 July 1804
Territorial Papers of the US - volume: 9 page: 257
Sauve, Orleans Territory, New Orleans
Sauve, Male
Petition, 17 Sep 1804, by inhabitants & colonists of LA to Gov. Claiborne, requesting a commission be established for fear of a slave revolt.
Territorial Papers of the US - volume: 9 page: 296
Scott, Jos, Orleans Territory, New Orleans
Scott, Jos, Male
Recommendation, 1 Sept 1804, of William Brown as Collector by the subscribers, merchants, traders, and others of New Orleans
Territorial Papers of the US - volume: 9 page: 290
Seizen, Selistin, Orleans Territory
Seizen, Selistin, Male
Petition, 9 Nov 1804, by inhabitants of Pointe Coupee to Gov. Claiborne, requesting military aid because of fears of a slave revolt.
Territorial Papers of the US - volume: 9 page: 327
Sezan, Gorge, Orleans Territory
Sezan, Gorge, Male
Petition, 9 Nov 1804, by inhabitants of Pointe Coupee to Gov. Claiborne, requesting military aid because of fears of a slave revolt.
Territorial Papers of the US - volume: 9 page: 327
Sibley, John, Orleans Territory, Natchitoches
Sibley, John, Male **Job:** Doctor
Born in: America
Persons recommended by Governor Claiborne for members of the Legislative Council of the Orleans Territory, 17 August 1804.

Territorial Papers of the US - volume: 9 page: 277
Simon, Charles,   Orleans Territory
          Simon, Charles,   Male   **Color:**
          Colored
Address from the free people of color Jan. 1804,
volunteering for military service
Territorial Papers of the US - volume: 9 page: 175
Simon, Louis, Orleans Territory
          Simon, Louis, Male   **Color:** Colored
Address from the free people of color Jan. 1804,
volunteering for military service
Territorial Papers of the US - volume: 9 page: 174
Sorapurie,   Orleans Territory, New Orleans
          Sorapurie,   Male
Petition, 17 Sep 1804, by inhabitants & colonists
of LA to Gov. Claiborne, requesting a commission
be established for fear of a slave revolt.
Territorial Papers of the US - volume: 9 page: 296
Soulie, Jn,   Orleans Territory, New Orleans
          Soulie, Jn,   Male   **Job:**   Merchant
Memorial to Congress from merchants of New
Orleans, 9 Jan 1804, offering allegiance to the US
Territorial Papers of the US - volume: 9 page: 158
Soulier, L.,   Orleans Territory, New Orleans
          Soulier, L.,   Male   **Job:**   Merchant
Characterization of New Orleans residents, 1 July
1804
Territorial Papers of the US - volume: 9 page: 254
Soutier,   Orleans Territory, New Orleans
          Soutier,   Male
Characterization of New Orleans residents, 1 July
1804
Territorial Papers of the US - volume: 9 page: 251
Spencer, O. H.,   Orleans Territory, New
Orleans
          Spencer, O. H., Male
Recommendation, 1 Sept 1804, of William Brown
as Collector by the subscribers, merchants, traders,
and others of New Orleans
Territorial Papers of the US - volume: 9 page: 290
Spitzer, B. S., Orleans Territory, New Orleans
          Spitzer, B. S.,   Male   & Company
Recommendation, 1 Sept 1804, of William Brown
as Collector by the subscribers, merchants, traders,
and others of New Orleans
Territorial Papers of the US - volume: 9 page: 290
Sr Charlote De Ste Therese,   Orleans Territory,
New Orleans
          Sr Charlote De Ste Therese,   Female

Ursuline Nuns to the President, 23 Apr 1804,
seeking ratification of prior claim
Territorial Papers of the US - volume: 9 page: 232
Sr Christine De St Andre,   Orleans Territory,
New Orleans
          Sr Christine De St Andre,   Female
Ursuline Nuns to the President, 23 Apr 1804,
seeking ratification of prior claim
Territorial Papers of the US - volume: 9 page: 232
Sr De Ste Felicite Alzas,   Orleans Territory,
New Orleans
          Sr De Ste Felicite Alzas,   Female
Ursuline Nuns to the President, 23 Apr 1804,
seeking ratification of prior claim
Territorial Papers of the US - volume: 9 page: 232
Sr De Ste Marie Olivier,   Orleans Territory,
New Orleans
          Sr De Ste Marie Olivier,   Female
          Job: Assistant
Ursuline Nuns to the President, 23 Apr 1804,
seeking ratification of prior claim
Territorial Papers of the US - volume: 9 page: 232
Sr Emelie De St Francois,   Orleans Territory,
New Orleans
          Sr Emelie De St Francois,   Female
Ursuline Nuns to the President, 23 Apr 1804,
seeking ratification of prior claim
Territorial Papers of the US - volume: 9 page: 232
Sr Felicite Dt St Jean, Orleans Territory, New
Orleans
          Sr Felicite Dt St Jean,   Female
          "Novice"
Ursuline Nuns to the President, 23 Apr 1804,
seeking ratification of prior claim
Territorial Papers of the US - volume: 9 page: 232
Sr Margerite De St Charle-,   Orleans Territory,
New Orleans
          Sr Margerite De St Charle-,   Female
Ursuline Nuns to the President, 23 Apr 1804,
seeking ratification of prior claim
Territorial Papers of the US - volume: 9 page: 232
Sr Marie de Ste Madelaine,   Orleans Territory,
New Orleans
          Sr Marie de Ste Madelaine,   Female
Ursuline Nuns to the President, 23 Apr 1804,
seeking ratification of prior claim
Territorial Papers of the US - volume: 9 page: 232
Sr Marie Joseph Brauxe,   Orleans Territory,
New Orleans
          Sr Marie Joseph Brauxe,   Female

Ursuline Nuns to the President, 23 Apr 1804, seeking ratification of prior claim
Territorial Papers of the US - volume: 9 page: 232

Sr Marthe De St Antoine-, Orleans Territory, New Orleans
    Sr Marthe De St Antoine-, Female
Ursuline Nuns to the President, 23 Apr 1804, seeking ratification of prior claim
Territorial Papers of the US - volume: 9 page: 232

Sr Rosalie De Ste Scolastique, Orleans Territory, New Orleans
    Sr Rosalie De Ste Scolastique, Female
Ursuline Nuns to the President, 23 Apr 1804, seeking ratification of prior claim
Territorial Papers of the US - volume: 9 page: 232

Sr Therese De St Xavier Farjon, Orleans Territory, New Orleans
    Sr Therese De St Xavier Farjon, Female **Job:** "Superieure"
Ursuline Nuns to the President, 23 Apr 1804, seeking ratification of prior claim
Territorial Papers of the US - volume: 9 page: 232

Stille, James, Orleans Territory, New Orleans
    Stille, James, Male
Recommendation, 1 Sept 1804, of William Brown as Collector by the subscribers, merchants, traders, and others of New Orleans
Territorial Papers of the US - volume: 9 page: 290

Tounoirs, J. Bte, Orleans Territory
    Tounoirs, J. Bte, Male
Petition, 9 Nov 1804, by inhabitants of Pointe Coupee to Gov. Claiborne, requesting military aid because of fears of a slave revolt.
Territorial Papers of the US - volume: 9 page: 327

Touro, Orleans Territory, New Orleans
    Touro, Male Partner of Judas
Recommendation, 1 Sept 1804, of William Brown as Collector by the subscribers, merchants, traders, and others of New Orleans
Territorial Papers of the US - volume: 9 page: 290

Towles, John, Orleans Territory
    Towles, John, Male
Petition, 9 Nov 1804, by inhabitants of Pointe Coupee to Gov. Claiborne, requesting military aid because of fears of a slave revolt.
Territorial Papers of the US - volume: 9 page: 326

Tremoulet, B., Orleans Territory, New Orleans
    Tremoulet, B., Male

Petition, 17 Sep 1804, by inhabitants & colonists of LA to Gov. Claiborne, requesting a commission be established for fear of a slave revolt.
Territorial Papers of the US - volume: 9 page: 296

Tricou, Jh, Orleans Territory, New Orleans
    Tricou, Jh, Male **Job:** Merchant
Memorial to Congress from merchants of New Orleans, 9 Jan 1804, offering allegiance to the US
Territorial Papers of the US - volume: 9 page: 158

Tricou, Jh, Orleans Territory, New Orleans
    Tricou, Jh, Male
Recommendation, 1 Sept 1804, of William Brown as Collector by the subscribers, merchants, traders, and others of New Orleans
Territorial Papers of the US - volume: 9 page: 290

Trudeaux, Valfroy, Orleans Territory
    Trudeaux, Valfroy, Male **Color:** Colored
Address from the free people of color Jan. 1804, volunteering for military service
Territorial Papers of the US - volume: 9 page: 174

Tupper, Benjn, Orleans Territory, New Orleans
    Tupper, Benjn, Male
Recommendation, 1 Sept 1804, of William Brown as Collector by the subscribers, merchants, traders, and others of New Orleans
Territorial Papers of the US - volume: 9 page: 290

Urquhart, T. D., Orleans Territory, New Orleans
    Urquhart, T. D., Male
Recommendation, 1 Sept 1804, of William Brown as Collector by the subscribers, merchants, traders, and others of New Orleans
Territorial Papers of the US - volume: 9 page: 290

Urquhart, T. J.D., Orleans Territory, New Orleans
    Urquhart, T. J.D., Male **Job:** Merchant
Memorial to Congress from merchants of New Orleans, 9 Jan 1804, offering allegiance to the US
Territorial Papers of the US - volume: 9 page: 158

Urquhart, Thomas, Orleans Territory, New Orleans
    Urquhart, Thomas, 30 Male **Job:** merchant "a Creole of the Country . . . educated in England"
Characterization of New Orleans residents, 1 July 1804
Territorial Papers of the US - volume: 9 page: 255

V--alin, Orleans Territory
V--alin, Male **Color:** Colored
Address from the free people of color Jan. 1804, volunteering for military service
Territorial Papers of the US - volume: 9 page: 174

Vige, Guebo Fs, Orleans Territory
Vige, Guebo Fs, Male
Petition, 9 Nov 1804, by inhabitants of Pointe Coupee to Gov. Claiborne, requesting military aid because of fears of a slave revolt.
Territorial Papers of the US - volume: 9 page: 327

Villain, Nicolas, Orleans Territory
Villain, Nicolas, Male
Petition, 9 Nov 1804, by inhabitants of Pointe Coupee to Gov. Claiborne, requesting military aid because of fears of a slave revolt.
Territorial Papers of the US - volume: 9 page: 327

Viriart, Orleans Territory
Viriart, Male
Petition, 9 Nov 1804, by inhabitants of Pointe Coupee to Gov. Claiborne, requesting military aid because of fears of a slave revolt.
Territorial Papers of the US - volume: 9 page: 327

Voisin, Josephe j. Bte, Orleans Territory
Voisin, Josephe j. Bte, Male **Color:** Colored
Address from the free people of color Jan. 1804, volunteering for military service
Territorial Papers of the US - volume: 9 page: 175

Watkins, Jno, Orleans Territory, New Orleans
Watkins, Jno, Male
Recommendation, 1 Sept 1804, of William Brown as Collector by the subscribers, merchants, traders, and others of New Orleans
Territorial Papers of the US - volume: 9 page: 290

Watkins, John, Orleans Territory, New Orleans
Watkins, John, Male **Job:** Doctor
Persons recommended by Governor Claiborne for members of the Legislative Council of the Orleans Territory, 17 August 1804.
Territorial Papers of the US - volume: 9 page: 277

Welboan, Wm B, Orleans Territory
Welboan, Wm B, Male
Petition, 9 Nov 1804, by inhabitants of Pointe Coupee to Gov. Claiborne, requesting military aid because of fears of a slave revolt.
Territorial Papers of the US - volume: 9 page: 326

West, Benja. F., Orleans Territory, New Orleans

West, Benja. F., Male
Recommendation, 1 Sept 1804, of William Brown as Collector by the subscribers, merchants, traders, and others of New Orleans
Territorial Papers of the US - volume: 9 page: 290

Wikoff, Orleans Territory, New Orleans
Wikoff, Male "of the Appalousa an American . . . fortune and influence . . . among the most early settlers, ignorant"
Characterization of New Orleans residents, 1 July 1804
Territorial Papers of the US - volume: 9 page: 256

Williamson, Orleans Territory, New Orleans
Williamson, Male Partner of Meeker & Patton
Recommendation, 1 Sept 1804, of William Brown as Collector by the subscribers, merchants, traders, and others of New Orleans
Territorial Papers of the US - volume: 9 page: 290

Williamson, Orleans Territory, New Orleans
Williamson, Male **Job:** Merchant
Business partner of Meeker & Patton
Memorial to Congress from merchants of New Orleans, 9 Jan 1804, offering allegiance to the US
Territorial Papers of the US - volume: 9 page: 158

Winter, Orleans Territory, New Orleans
Winter, Male Partner of Harman
Recommendation, 1 Sept 1804, of William Brown as Collector by the subscribers, merchants, traders, and others of New Orleans
Territorial Papers of the US - volume: 9 page: 290

Wykoff, William, Orleans Territory, St. Landry
Wykoff, William, Male
"American of wealth"
Persons recommended by Governor Claiborne for members of the Legislative Council of the Orleans Territory, 17 August 1804.
Territorial Papers of the US - volume: 9 page: 277

Wykoff, William, Jr. Orleans Territory, Opposite Baton Rouge
Wykoff, William, Jr. Male "a long time merchant in the City, and now retired to a valuable plantation"
Persons recommended by Governor Claiborne for members of the Legislative Council of the Orleans Territory, 17 August 1804.
Territorial Papers of the US - volume: 9 page: 278

Young, Samuel, Orleans Territory, Pointe Coupee

Young, Samuel,   Male **Job:**
Planter "rich"
Persons recommended by Governor Claiborne for
members of the Legislative Council of the Orleans
Territory, 17 August 1804.
Territorial Papers of the US - volume: 9 page: 278
Zacharie,   Orleans Territory, New Orleans
          Zacharie,   Male   Partner of Holmes
Recommendation, 1 Sept 1804, of William Brown
as Collector by the subscribers, merchants, traders,
and others of New Orleans
Territorial Papers of the US - volume: 9 page: 290
Zacharie, Stephen,   Orleans Territory,   New
Orleans
          Zacharie, Stephen,   Male **Job:**
Merchant

Memorial to Congress from merchants of New
Orleans, 9 Jan 1804, offering allegiance to the US
Territorial Papers of the US - volume: 9 page: 158
Zackarie,   Orleans Territory, New Orleans
          Zackarie,   Male **Job:** Merchant
Business partner of Holmes
Memorial to Congress from merchants of New
Orleans, 9 Jan 1804, offering allegiance to the US
Territorial Papers of the US - volume: 9 page: 158
Zerban, Philip,   Orleans   Territory,   New
Orleans
          Zerban, Philip, Male
Recommendation, 1 Sept 1804, of William Brown
as Collector by the subscribers, merchants, traders,
and others of New Orleans
Territorial Papers of the US - volume: 9 page: 290

STEMMONS PUBLISHING, 1078 Shields Lane, South Jordan, Utah 84095, 801-254-2152
(Call between 9:00 a.m. and 5:00 p.m. Monday through Friday. If no one answers, please leave a
message.), stemmonspublishing@gmail.com

The importance of census records and other population lists cannot be overstated in terms of the help they are in
locating people in a specific area. This allows one to examine other records in that area. This is one of our main
goals and why we do business. What we are trying to accomplish is a work in progress. We hope to improve as we
go along. Thank you for your patience.

Petitions are an important example of these population lists.

Thank you for the opportunity to serve you.

Sincerely,
John Stemmons

A COMPLETE LIST OF OUR GENEALOGY BOOKS

AL-01 **ALABAMA 1800 PETITIONERS [-1804]**© Compiled by
John D Stemmons, 2021. This book compiled from *Territorial Papers
of the United States* contains 253 entries for a very early period in
Alabama's history. It may contain some biographical details and clues
to prior residence. It can help substitute for the missing federal census.
For information on how to obtain this book search by the title or
"Books by John Stemmons" at Amazon.com. This comes
automatically with a paperback binding. It includes but is not limited
to petitions regarding:
- Seeking new territory due to the rapid migration from
  Georgia, etc.
- Petition seeking confirmation of land grants obtained from
  other governments.

36 Pages $7.20

AL-02 **ALABAMA 1810 PETITIONERS, ETC., [1805-1814]**©
Compiled by John D Stemmons, 2021. This book compiled from
Territorial Papers of the United States contains 1687 entries for a

very early period in Alabama's history. It includes a census of
Madison County, taken Jan 1809. It may contain some biographical
details and clues to prior residence. It can help substitute for the
missing federal census. For information on how to obtain this book
search by the title or "Books by John Stemmons" at Amazon.com.
This comes automatically with a paperback binding. It includes but is
not limited to petitions regarding:
- Issues relating to land.
- Petition of inhabitants east of Pearl River seeking to form a
  new territory.
- 1809 census of Madison County.
- Inhabitants of Tombigbee seeking for their purchases from
  the Spanish to be duty free at "Fort Stoddart".

176 Pages $35.20

AL-03 **ALABAMA 1820 PETITIONERS, ETC., [1815-1824]**©
Compiled by John D Stemmons, 2021. This book compiled from
Territorial Papers of the United States contains 3913 entries for a

fast-growing period in Alabama's history. It may contain some biographical details and clues to prior residence. It can help substitute for the missing federal census. For information on how to obtain this book search by the title or "Books by John Stemmons" at Amazon.com. This comes automatically with a paperback binding. It includes but is not limited to petitions regarding:

- Merchants and traders of St. Stephens seeking to establish that town as a port of delivery.
- Inhabitants of eastern part of MS territory, who lost much income/property in the wars with England & Indians.
- Inhabitants of Alabama Territory opposing the "settlements on the western side of the Mobile & Tombigby rivers" being made part of Mississippi.
- List of Letters, 9 Jan 1819, remaining in Huntsville Post Office.
- Issues about military and local officers.
- Memorial, ref. 20 Jan 1817, to Congress from inhabitants of Mobile complaining that Ft Charlotte is indefensible.

407 Pages $81.40

AR-01 **ARKANSAS PETITIONERS, ETC. 1800, 1810 [1795-1814]**© Compiled by John D Stemmons, 2021. This book compiled from *Territorial Papers of the United States* contains 261 entries and is a partial replacement for the missing federal censuses of 1800 and 1810. As a result, it is a very helpful resource in establishing residence of people in Arkansas during that early formative period in the state's history. These people include some of earliest you will find that established the foundation of what was to become the great state that Arkansas now is. This also makes it possible to determine what other records might be available for further research. Some additional biographical details may be included, and possible relationships with others may be revealed. For information on how to obtain this book search by the title or "Books by John Stemmons" at Amazon.com. This comes automatically with a paperback binding. It includes but is not limited to petitions regarding:

- Issues relating to land.
- Inhabitants of Arkansas District expressing concern about the hostile attitude of the Cherokees nearby.
- Issues about military and local officers.

43 Pages $8.60

AR-02 **ARKANSAS PETITIONERS, ETC. 1820 [1815-1824]**© Compiled by John D Stemmons, 2021. This book compiled from *Territorial Papers of the United States* contains 1936 entries and is a partial replacement for the missing federal census of 1820. As a result, it is a very helpful resource in establishing residence of people in Arkansas during that fast-growing territorial period prior to becoming a state. Unfortunately, the 1820 census is not available to help track these people. That is why this new book can help. It is even better in some respects than the census because it helps us understand some of the challenges they faced. It also makes possible the determination of other records that might be available for further research. Some additional biographical details may be included, and possible relationships with others may be revealed. Even the names of some Native Americans are included as well as a few potential residents of Oklahoma. For information on how to obtain this book search by the title or "Books by John Stemmons" at Amazon.com. This comes automatically with a paperback binding. It includes but is not limited to petitions regarding:

- Issues relating to land.
- Issues relating to Native Americans.
- Citizens of Arkansas County describing the good location of the Town of Arkansas.
- Appointments about military and local officers, etc.
- Inhabitants of Arkansas and Phillips Counties seeking a mail route from the Town of Arkansas to the "Post of Ouachita in Louisianna."

Abstract of Grand and Petit Jurors, Oct term, 1824 listing compensation for their attendance at a Superior Court held at Little Rock.

216 Pages $43.20

1001-**GEORGIA PETITIONS 1778-1784**© Compiled by John D Stemmons, 2004. This book contains 256 entries for a very early period in Georgia's history. For information on how to obtain this book search by the title or "Books by John Stemmons" at Amazon.com. This comes automatically with a paperback binding. It includes but is not limited to petitions regarding:

- A desire for a new district.
- A request for local courts.
- Issues about military and local officers.
- Request for protection against enemies.
- A request for pardon, amnesty, etc.
- Description of hardship.

44 pages $8.80

1002-**GEORGIA PETITIONS 1785-1794**© Compiled by John D Stemmons, 2004. Contains 3720 entries which includes about 25% of the heads of household in Georgia at that time. As such this publication is an excellent substitute for the missing Georgia 1790 federal census. It even includes many names for Burke and Washington Counties which suffered severe record loss in the early years. For information on how to obtain this book search by the title or "Books by John Stemmons" at Amazon.com. This comes automatically with a paperback binding. It includes but is not limited to petitions regarding:

- Issues regarding local agencies, boundary changes, etc.
- Issues regarding religion and churches.
- Issues about military and local officers.
- Asking for measures to control slaves.
- Recommendation for a business opportunity.
- Seeking resolution of land problems, land fraud, etc.
- Asking for increased tobacco inspection fees.
- Request for protection against Indians.
- Issues about crimes, pardon, amnesty, etc.
- Description of hardship.

367 pages $73.40

IL-01 **ILLINOIS PETITIONS, ETC., 1760-1810 [1755-1814]**© Compiled by John D Stemmons, 2021, this book contains 3680 names from *The Territorial Papers of the U.S.* This covers a period of time even before the federal census of 1790. And while no federal censuses exists for Illinois from 1790-1810, these records nicely substitute for those missing documents. It should be noted that 1004-**A PARTIAL CENSUS FOR INDIANA TERRITORY 1810** includes most if not all the names for 1810. A study to determine that they were the same was inconclusive and so, just in the outside chance there might be some that were not the same, it was felt that they should be included. The convenience of having them together outweighs their exclusion. These records include an incredible amount of information about these early people. One can see the change from a mostly French culture to that of English. The transition was not always peaceful. Included are census records, lists of inhabitants, and much more. While the federal censuses are missing that would help track these people, these records are even better in some respects than the census because it helps us understand some of the challenges they faced. That is why this new book can help. Some additional biographical details may be included, plus possible relationships with other family members. For information on how to obtain this book search by the title or "Books by John Stemmons" at Amazon.com. This comes automatically with a paperback binding. It includes but is not limited to petitions regarding:

- Issues relating to land.
- Issues relating to Native Americans.
- List of inhabitants at Kaskaskias before 1783.
- Appointments about military and local officers, etc.

- Lands claimed and possessed by inhabitants of the District of Cahokia on or before 1783 that still existed after 29 May 1790.
- Applications for lands in the District of Cahokia by persons claiming as settlers under the state of Virginia, if the settlements were made on or before 1783 that still existed after 29 May 1790.
- List of families at the Prairie du Pont, undated, but enclosed in St. Clair's report 10 Feb 1791.

349 Pages $69.80

IN-01 THE TERRITORY NORTHWEST OF THE RIVER OHIO, PETITIONERS, ETC., 1790-1800 [1785-1804] (Present day Indiana)© Compiled by John D Stemmons, 2021. This book was compiled from *Territorial Papers of the United States.* 1790 contains 242 names found on petitions, etc., including a census of heads of household for Vincennes. 1800 only includes 76 names and so is not as valuable as 1790. The population of Indiana would have increased significantly between 1790 and 1800. This is still a very early time prior to Indiana becoming a state. Unfortunately, there is no 1790 or 1800 census existing to help track these people. Therefore, we must do what we can with what is available. That is why this new book is so helpful. It is even better in some respects than the census because it helps us understand some of the challenges they faced. It also makes possible the determination of other records that might be available for further research such as land grants. Even the names of some Native Americans are listed. Some additional biographical details may be included, plus possible relationships with other family members. For information on how to obtain this book search by the title or "Books by John Stemmons" at Amazon.com. This comes automatically with a paperback binding. It includes but is not limited to petitions regarding:

- Issues relating to land.
- Heads of families settled at Post Vincennes on or before 1783 and residents at this time [13 Jul 1790] who are entitled to donation lands.
- Issues relating to Native Americans.
- Inhabitants of Vincennes who migrated to Vincennes around 1786 and received land, but never obtained a deed.
- Appointments about military and local officers, etc.

38 Pages $7.60

1003-INDIANA ELECTION RETURNS 1809, 1812© Compiled by John D and E. Diane Stemmons, 2004. This compilation of 3576 entries includes the names found in the territorial election returns which documents are in the Indiana Historical Society. Also included is a poll book of an election for Dearborn County in 1809 as found in *Territorial Papers of the United States*. All entries in this book are also found in *A Partial Census for Indiana Territory 1810*. The book *Indiana Election Returns, 1809, 1812* was compiled for just the election returns simply because they are one entire record source and may have some value in that. For information on how to obtain this book search by the title or "Books by John Stemmons" at Amazon.com. This comes automatically with a paperback binding.

285 pages $57.00

1004-A PARTIAL CENSUS FOR INDIANA TERRITORY 1810© Compiled by John D and E. Diane Stemmons, 2021. With 8602 entries this book includes name lists found in *Territorial Papers of the United States* for Indiana Territory during the period 1805 through 1814. It also provides the names in *Indiana Election Returns 1809, 1812* listed above. Since there were approximately 4300 heads of households in the territory in 1810, *A Partial Census for Indiana Territory 1810* probably lists virtually every head of household in Indiana Territory for the time period. It makes an excellent substitute for the missing federal census for 1810. In addition, it includes names of people living in what is now Illinois, but which was part of Indiana Territory before 1809. Therefore, *A Partial Census for Indiana Territory 1810* is also a partial census of Illinois in the years between

1805 to 1809. For information on how to obtain this book search by the title or "Books by John Stemmons" at Amazon.com. This comes automatically with a paperback binding. It includes but is not limited to petitions regarding:

- Issues relating to land.
- Heads of families settled at Post Vincennes on or before 1783 and residents at this time [13 Jul 1790] who are entitled to donation lands.
- Issues relating to Native Americans.
- Inhabitants of Vincennes who migrated to Vincennes around 1786 and received land, but never obtained a deed.
- Appointments about military and local officers, etc.

574 pages $114.80

KY-01 KENTUCKY 1800, BARREN COUNTY TAX BOOK© Compiled by John D Stemmons, 2021. It contains 494 names from the Barren County tax list and 1 from *The Territorial Papers of the U.S.* Even though the 1800 census is missing this list it provides an amazing amount of information that substitutes nicely for that missing census, including white and black males aged 16-21 and those 21 and over. This is the kind of information one would expect to find on the census for that period. This list includes all taxable heads of household. Some additional biographical details may be included, plus possible relationships with other family members. The names of the blacks may be found in court, land, and probate records. For information on how to obtain this book search by the title or "Books by John Stemmons" at Amazon.com. This comes automatically with a paperback binding.

65 Pages $13.00

LA-01 ARKANSAS PETITIONS 1800 [1795-1804] and ORLEANS TERRITORY (NOW LOUISIANA) PETITIONS, ETC., 1800 [1795-1804]© Compiled by John D Stemmons, 2021. This book was compiled from *Territorial Papers of the United States* and contains 495 names for Louisiana and 3 from Arkansas. Since no federal census exists for Arkansas and Louisiana for 1800, these records nicely substitute for those missing documents. These records include an incredible amount of information about these early people. While the federal censuses are missing that would help track these people, these records are even better in some respects than the census because it helps us understand some of the challenges they faced. That is why this new book can help. Some additional biographical details may be included, plus possible relationships with other family members. For information on how to obtain this book search by the title or "Books by John Stemmons" at Amazon.com. This comes automatically with a paperback binding. It includes but is not limited to petitions regarding:

- Inhabitants of Pointe Coupee to Gov. Claiborne, requesting military aid because of fears of a slave revolt.
- Characterization of New Orleans residents, 1 July 1804.
- Address from the free people of color Jan. 1804, volunteering for military service.
- Memorial to Congress from merchants of New Orleans, 9 Jan 1804, offering allegiance to the US.
- Appointments about military and local officers, etc.

47 Pages $9.40

MO-01 MISSOURI PETITIONERS, ETC., 1780-1820 [1775-1824]© Compiled by John D Stemmons, 2021. This book was compiled from *Territorial Papers of the United States* and contains 1 name for 1780, 12 names for 1790, 19 names for 1800, 5057 names for 1810, and 1509 names for 1820. The later lists begin to approach the number needed to include most heads of household, and nicely substitute for missing or no censuses. These records include an incredible amount of information about these early people. While censuses help track people, the records this book includes are even better in some respects than the census because it helps us understand some of their personal feelings and challenges, they faced. Some additional biographical details may be included, plus possible relationships with other family members. For information on how to obtain this book search by the title or "Books by John Stemmons" at Amazon.com. This comes automatically with a paperback binding. It includes but is not limited to petitions, etc., regarding:

- Resolution recommending distinction between Americans and Frenchmen should be done away.
- Letter from U.S. President to Chief White Hairs and the warriors of the Osages, informing them of the Lewis and Clark expedition, and promising them a resident agent.
- Many petitions, etc., expressing their support and confidence in Governor Wilkinson. He was involved in scandals and controversies.
- Memorial recommending replacements for Governor Wilkinson.
- Petition expressing concern about changing the form of territorial government before they are adequately prepared.
- Memorial concerning the large number of their Spanish land claims that are being rejected.
- Lists of civil and military officers.
- Petition seeking a grant of a township of land for the support of the school as had been done in other areas.
- Petition seeking pre-emption rights for the services given in defending the frontier in Boon's Lick Settlement around 1815.
- Petitions relating to the New Madrid & Little Prairie earthquake.
- Petitions asking for new post offices and routes, etc.

552 pages$110.40

MI-01 MICHIGAN PETITIONS, ETC. 1790-1810 [1785-1814]© Compiled by John D Stemmons, 2021. This book was compiled from *Territorial Papers of the United States*. It contains 1 name for 1790, 794 names for 1800, and 1335 names for 1810. Clearly, that is not enough for 1790, but the others begin to approach the number needed. Especially is this so for 1810 because we are fortunate enough to have much of what appears to be the federal 1810 census. Since no federal census exists for 1800, these records nicely substitute for those missing documents. These records include an incredible amount of information about these early people. While censuses help track people, the records this book includes are even better in some respects than the census because it helps us understand some of their personal feelings and challenges, they faced. Some additional biographical details may be included, plus possible relationships with other family members. For information on how to obtain this book search by the title or "Books by John Stemmons" at Amazon.com. This comes automatically with a paperback binding. It includes but is not limited to petitions regarding:

- Inhabitants of Detroit seeking new territory because of distance to travel to the headquarters of Indiana Territory.
- Appointments about military and local officers, etc.
- Inhabitants of Wayne County seeking clarification of the status of their land.
- 1810 Census of the District of Detroit.
- Inhabitants of Michigan Ter. seeking time to file claims to their land.
- List, 23 Jul 1812, of patents received from the General Land Office for private claims in the District of Detroit.
- Petition from inhabitants of Michigan Territory asking that the new territorial code be printed also in French.
- Petition to Thomas Jefferson, from inhabitants of Michigan Territory complaining of Governor William Hull and Supreme Court Chief Justice Augustus B. Woodward.

222 Pages$44.40

MS-01 MISSISSIPPI TERRITORIAL PETITIONERS, ETC. 1800 [1795-1804]© Compiled by John D Stemmons, 2021. This book was compiled from *Territorial Papers of the United States and*

contains 2566 names found on petitions, etc., from Mississippi Territory for this time period. This was during a fast-growing era prior to Mississippi becoming a state. Unfortunately, there is no 1800 census existing to help track these people. That is why this new book can help. It is even better in some respects than the census because it helps us understand some of the challenges they faced. It also makes possible the determination of other records that might be available for further research such as Spanish land grants. Some additional biographical details may be included, plus possible relationships with other family members. For information on how to obtain this book search by the title or "Books by John Stemmons" at Amazon.com. This comes automatically with a paperback binding. It includes but is not limited to petitions regarding:

- Citizens of territory asking land office to be in the area, settlers have pre-emption right, & suffrage be for males of age and US citizens & residents of territory for 6 months.
- Memorial by citizens of the territory, who obtained land before the area became part of the US.
- Testimonials, ca 1802, by individuals regarding the service of John Steele, secretary of the territory.
- Memorial by citizens of the territory seeking that "moderate grants [be] made to actual settlers on unappropriated lands,"
- Merchants of Natchez, complaining of the extra duties they must pay for merchandise shipped from the US.

209 Pages$41.80

MS-02 MISSISSIPPI TERRITORIAL PETITIONS, ETC. 1810 [1805-1814] and WEST FLORIDA 1820 PETITIONERS [1815-1824]© Compiled by John D Stemmons, 2021. This book was compiled from *Territorial Papers of the United States* and contains 1061 names found on petitions, etc., from Mississippi Territory for the period 1810 [1805-1814]. It also includes a list of 76 names on a petition to Congress, 11 Dec 1816, by inhabitants of Jackson County, Mississippi Territory, many of whom settled on land in West Florida while under Spanish control and now seek for their grant to be confirmed by the US. It is being included with Mississippi Territory because it is basically the same time period and place of residence. This was during a fast-growing time prior to Mississippi and Florida becoming states. Unfortunately, there is no 1810 or 1820 census existing to help track these people. That is why this new book can help. It is even better in some respects than the census because it helps us understand some of the challenges they faced. It also makes possible the determination of other records that might be available for further research. Some additional biographical details may be included, and possible relationships with others may be revealed. For information on how to obtain this book search by the title or "Books by John Stemmons" at Amazon.com. This comes automatically with a paperback binding. It includes but is not limited to petitions regarding:

- Inhabitants of the territory seeking adjustment of land claims obtained from the British Government.
- Inhabitants of the territory seek for a road to be built that follows the Pearl River which would shorten the route from Nashville to New Orleans.
- Inhabitants of Amite and Wilkinson Counties seek establishment of a post office.
- Memorial by citizens of the territory (Americans by birth?) seeking a postponement of statehood for the territory.
- Inhabitants of Jackson Co., Mississippi Territory, many of whom settled on land in West Florida while under Spanish control seek for their grant to be confirmed by the US.

108 Pages$21.60

NJ-01-NEW JERSEY PETITIONS 1740, 1745 THROUGH 1754© Compiled by John D Stemmons, 2021. It contains 740 entries for a period of time in New Jersey when records are sparse. While that may not seem like very many names, it was during the time when the population was small, and the residence of people was sometimes hard to track. In looking through these petitions, it appears that the people of this era had basically the same concerns we have. One can see the forces of democracy beginning to stir that were to result in independence from Great Britain just a short three decades away. We can obtain a hint of the personal concerns of these people and what was important to them in this exciting historical time. Even at this time of great distress and hardship life had to go on. These petitions are almost like an open window into the lives of these people. For information on how to obtain this book search by the title or "Books by John Stemmons" at Amazon.com. This comes automatically with a paperback binding. It includes but is not limited to petitions regarding:

- Issues regarding exports and imports.
- Issues regarding devaluation of currency, money supply, etc.
- Issues regarding local agencies, boundary changes, etc.
- Seeking new legislation.
- Issues about military and government officers.
- Seeking resolution of land problems, etc.
- Protesting against the great number of taverns.
- Resolution of tax issues.
- Issues about crimes, pardon, amnesty, etc.

84 pages $16.80

NJ-02-NEW JERSEY PETITIONS 1755-1764© Compiled by John D Stemmons, 2004. Contains 2389 entries from many petitions submitted because of concerns about the French and Indian War. This book is an excellent census substitute. For information on how to obtain this book search by the title or "Books by John Stemmons" at Amazon.com. This comes automatically with a paperback binding. It includes petitions regarding:

- Issues regarding local agencies, boundary changes, etc.
- Issues about roads, bridges, etc.
- Opposition to importing slaves.
- Seeking naturalization.
- Seeking new legislation.
- Issues about military and government affairs.
- Request for reimbursement from the government.
- Request for protection against enemies.
- Seeking resolution of land problems, etc.
- Protesting against dispensing of "spirituous liquors"
- Issues about crimes, pardon, amnesty, etc.
- Description of hardship.

246 pages $49.20

NJ-03-NEW JERSEY PETITIONS 1765-1774© Compiled by John D Stemmons, 2004. This book contains 806 entries. While a small percent of the population, it represents the time leading up to the Revolution. For information on how to obtain this book search by the title or "Books by John Stemmons" at Amazon.com. This comes automatically with a paperback binding. It includes but is not limited to petitions regarding:

- Issues regarding agriculture, exports and imports.
- Request for permission to beg, financial support, etc.
- Issues about religion and churches.
- Request for medical standards.
- Issues regarding devaluation of currency, money supply, etc.
- Issues regarding local agencies, boundary changes, etc.
- Issues on hunting, fishing, etc.
- Issues about roads, bridges, etc.
- Issues relating to slavery.
- Issues about military and government affairs.
- Seeking resolution of land problems, etc.
- Issues about crimes, pardon, amnesty, etc.

99 pages $19.80

NJ-04-**NEW JERSEY PETITIONS 1775-1784**© Compiled by John D Stemmons, 2005. This book contains 6201 entries which is about 29% of the heads of household living in New Jersey at that time (not counting duplicate names.) It represents the historic period during the Revolution. For information on how to obtain this book search by the title or "Books by John Stemmons" at Amazon.com. This comes automatically with a paperback binding. It includes but is not limited to petitions regarding:

- Issues regarding trade, exports, and imports.
- Issues regarding devaluation of currency, money supply, price controls, etc.
- Issues on religion and churches.
- Issues regarding local agencies, boundary changes or disputes, etc.
- Issues on court cases.
- Request for guardianship of children.
- Issues about roads, bridges, canals, etc.
- Issues on slavery.
- Seeking new legislation or repealing old laws.
- Issues about military and government affairs and officers.
- Issues about payment from the government.
- Issues on independence and the Revolutionary War.
- Request for protection against enemies.
- Seeking resolution of property and land problems, etc.
- Issues about crimes, pardon, amnesty, etc.
- Resolution of tax issues.

559 pages $111.80

NJ-05-**NEW JERSEY PETITIONS 1785-1794 Volumes 1-2**© Compiled by John D Stemmons, 2005. This book contains 10,353 entries which covers about 35% of the heads of household for that time, not counting duplicate names. For information on how to obtain this book search by the title or "Books by John Stemmons" at Amazon.com. This comes automatically with a paperback binding. It includes but is not limited to petitions regarding:

- Economic issues regarding the devaluation of currency, public debt, etc.
- Issues on religion and churches.
- Issues regarding counties and towns, etc.
- Issues on court cases.
- Issues regarding hunting on private property, fishing, etc.
- Issues about roads, bridges, canals, ferries, etc.
- Issues relating to schools.
- Issues on slavery.
- Seeking new legislation or repealing existing laws.
- Issues about military and government affairs and officers.
- Seeking payment from the government.
- Expressing approval of the U.S. Constitution.
- Seeking resolution of property and land problems, etc.
- Issues about crimes, pardon, amnesty, etc.
- Resolution of tax issues.

Volume 1, A Through K, pages 462 $92.40
Volume 2, L Through Z, pages 470 $94.00

NJ-06 NEW JERSEY PETITIONERS, ETC., 1800 [1795-1804] Volumes 1-3© Compiled by John Stemmons, 2021. All volumes of this book contain 13,144 names. Unlike the tax ratables, these records cover the entire state for the period just after the Revolutionary War These records provide a place of residence which can lead to other records to search. For information on how to obtain this book search by the title or "Books by John Stemmons" at Amazon.com. This comes automatically with a paperback binding. It includes but is not limited to petitions regarding:

- Public buildings including poor house, taverns, banks, etc.
- Issues on religion and churches.
- Issues regarding counties and towns, etc.
- Issues on court cases.

- Concerning voting opportunities
- Issues about roads, bridges, canals, ferries, water rights, storage of gunpowder, etc.
- Issues relating to schools.
- Issues on slavery.
- Seeking new legislation or repealing existing laws.
- Issues about military and government affairs and officers.
- Seeking payment from the government.
- Seeking resolution of property and land problems, etc.
- Issues about crimes, pardon, amnesty, etc.
- Resolution of tax issues.

Volume 1, A Through E, pages 423 $84.60
Volume 2, F Through R, pages 529 $105.80
Volume 3, S Through Z, pages 358 $71.60

NJ-07 NEW JERSEY TAX RATABLES, 1770 [1765-1774] This book contains 2373 names of those who are taxable. They do include important details about the property they held and may provide clues regarding relationship, etc. For information on how to obtain this book search by the title or "Books by John Stemmons" at Amazon.com. This comes automatically with a paperback binding.
250 pages $50.00

NJ-08 NEW JERSEY TAX RATABLES, 1780 [1775-1784] This book contains 4358 names of those who are taxable. It includes important details about the property they held and may provide clues regarding relationship, etc. For information on how to obtain this book search by the title or "Books by John Stemmons" at Amazon.com. This comes automatically with a paperback binding.
440 pages $88.00

NJ-09 NEW JERSEY TAX RATABLES, 1790 [1785-1794] This book contains 2307 names of those who are taxable. Unfortunately, Burlington and Cape May counties are not covered by this period. We are fortunate though in have the petitions that cover the same time. It is interesting to compare the two sets of records. They were not combined because that would make the books too large. The tax ratables do include important details about the property they held and may provide clues regarding relationship, etc. For information on how to obtain this book search by the title or "Books by John Stemmons" at Amazon.com. This comes automatically with a paperback binding.
268 pages $53.60

NJ-10 NEW JERSEY TAX RATABLES, 1800 [1795-1804] , Volumes 1-2 This book contains 8396 names of those who are taxable. It includes important details about the property they held and may provide clues regarding relationship, etc. For information on how to obtain this book search by the title or "Books by John Stemmons" at Amazon.com. This comes automatically with a paperback binding.
Volume 1, A Through K, pages 456 $91.20
Volume 2, L Through Z, pages 449 $89.80

NC-01 NORTH CAROLINA PETITIONERS, ETC. 1780 [1775-1784]© Compiled by John Stemmons, 2021. This book contains 4866 names and was assembled from records located at the North Carolina State Archives. This was before the federal census was taken and is a valuable resource for locating people in this early time. Included are some names from what is now, Tennessee. For information on how to obtain this book search by the title or "Books by John Stemmons" at Amazon.com. This comes automatically with a paperback binding.

- Economic issues regarding the devaluation of currency, public debt, etc.
- Issues on religion and churches.
- Issues regarding counties and towns, etc.
- Issues regarding hunting on private property, fishing, etc.
- Issues about roads, bridges, canals, ferries, etc.
- Seeking new legislation or repealing existing laws.
- Issues about military and government affairs and officers.

- Seeking resolution of property and land problems, etc.
- Issues about crimes, pardon, amnesty, etc.

568 pages $113.60

1009-ROWAN COUNTY, NORTH CAROLINA TAX LISTS 1758/1759, 1761, 1768, 1778, 1779© Compiled by John D and E. Diane Stemmons, 2004. This publication serves as a census for Rowan County for about three decades which includes two major conflicts, the French and Indian and Revolutionary wars. Thus, one may be able to track individuals that stayed in the county over a significant period of time. Sometimes sons and slaves are given plus other important information. These tax lists are listed alphabetically in three separate sections.
218 pages $43.60

OH-01 TERRITORY NW OF OHIO RIVER, PETITIONERS, ETC. 1790-1800 [1785-1804] (Now Ohio)© Compiled by John D Stemmons, 2021. It contains 217 names for 1790 and 3047 names for 1800. This book may include many heads of household at that time and serves as a substitute for missing or no censuses. It even incorporates the names of many native Americans. These records provide an incredible amount of information about these early people. While censuses help track people, the records this book contains are even better in some respects than the census because it helps us understand some of their personal information not recorded by a census. Some additional biographical details may be included, plus possible relationships with other family members. For information on how to obtain this book search by the title or "Books by John Stemmons" at Amazon.com. This comes automatically with a paperback binding. It includes but is not limited to petitions regarding:

- Petition of the French inhabitants of Gallipolis regarding their purchase of lands from the Scioto Company.
- Inhabitants on the Muskingum to Governor St. Clair.
- Petitions about land and issues with John Cleves Symmes.
- 1800, Population Schedules, Washington County. Territory Northwest of the River Ohio.
- Petition by inhabitants telling of losses in the "Late Indian war" and their inability to obtain land in Kentucky.
- Petition by inhabitants of Hamilton County seeking approval to purchase reserved land in order to build a grist mill because it has a sufficient stream of water.
- List of Gallipolis proprietors and the amount of their land purchases.

285 pages $57.00

PA-01 PENNSYLVANIA CHESTER COUNTY TAX LIST 1771© Compiled by John D Stemmons, 2021. It contains 5621 names. This record lists all taxable people in the county, and as such, is a good census substitute. It is not known what is meant by the abbreviations or "inmate". Perhaps they were incarcerated in jail or were indentured in some way. Often an occupation is listed. Occasionally there will be information about family relationships. It is helpful that this book includes the information about the taxable property. For information on how to obtain this book search by the title or "Books by John Stemmons" at Amazon.com. This comes automatically with a paperback binding.
399 pages $79.80

South Carolina

South Carolina has a remarkable series of records that makes it unique for the Colonial period. These are the "Jury Lists" compiled by the government to function as a list of names from which members of a jury could be assigned. They cover the period 1720-1783 and, according to the act in 1731, were compiled from tax lists of the preceding year [which no longer exist], listing every person who paid a tax of twenty shillings or more. Those who paid five pounds or more were listed as grand jurors. The poorer class of people would not be listed. While not a complete list of the heads of household, they represent a sizeable proportion. They serve as a census during a period of growth, migration, and war. Usually only the name is given, but sometimes an occupation or name of the father is listed, etc. Many names are on more than one list for a particular year.

1010-SOUTH CAROLINA 1720 JURY LIST© Compiled by John D and E. Diane Stemmons, 2004. This publication has 840 entries covering a time when South Carolina was only 50 years old and the population was very small with only an estimated 885 heads of household. Unfortunately, it does not list a residence other than South Carolina. For information on how to obtain this book search by the title or "Books by John Stemmons" at Amazon.com. This comes automatically with a paperback binding.
48 pages $9.60

1017-SOUTH CAROLINA 1731 JURY LIST© Compiled by John D and E. Diane Stemmons, 2005. This book contains 2160 entries. It lists the locality of every person. For information on how to obtain this book search by the title or "Books by John Stemmons" at Amazon.com. This comes automatically with a paperback binding.
110 pages $22.00

1011-SOUTH CAROLINA 1740 JURY LIST© Compiled by John D and E. Diane Stemmons, 2004. This book contains 2160 entries. It lists the locality of every person. For information on how to obtain this book search by the title or "Books by John Stemmons" at Amazon.com. This comes automatically with a paperback binding.
111 pages $22.20

1012-SOUTH CAROLINA 1751 JURY LIST© Compiled by John D and E. Diane Stemmons, 2004. This book contains 2170 entries. It lists the locality of every person. For information on how to obtain this book search by the title or "Books by John Stemmons" at Amazon.com. This comes automatically with a paperback binding.
109 pages $21.80

1013-SOUTH CAROLINA 1757 JURY LIST© Compiled by John D and E. Diane Stemmons, 2004. This book contains 2624 entries. It lists the locality of every person. For information on how to obtain this book search by the title or "Books by John Stemmons" at Amazon.com. This comes automatically with a paperback binding.
135 pages $27.00

1014-SOUTH CAROLINA 1767 JURY LIST© Compiled by John D and E. Diane Stemmons, 2004. This book contains 2385 entries. It lists the locality of every person. For information on how to obtain this book search by the title or "Books by John Stemmons" at Amazon.com. This comes automatically with a paperback binding.
127 pages $25.40

SC-07 SOUTH CAROLINA 1780 [1775-1784], VOLUMES 1-2© Compiled by John D Stemmons, 2021. It contains 13,444 names. This record of jury lists consist of many people during the Colonial/Revolutionary War period and as such, is a good census substitute. Since Loyalists owned property that they paid taxes on, they may be included as well. These records provide a place of residence which can lead to other records to search. For information on how to obtain this book search by the title or "Books by John Stemmons" at Amazon.com. This comes automatically with a paperback binding.
Volume 1, 502 pages $100.40
Volume 2, 575 pages $115.00

TN-01 TENNESSEE PETITIONS, ETC., 1770-1790 [1765-1794]© Also known as Territory South of Ohio River. Compiled by John Stemmons, 2021. This book was assembled from *Territorial Papers of the United States* and contains 1 name for 1770, 12 names for 1780, and 1161 names for 1790. These people listed seem to be the more prominent persons, so, most of the less noteworthy individuals would

not be listed. Still, the people listed clarify this early time before Tennessee became a state. The amount of biographical information is significant compared to the other books we have compiled from *Territorial Papers of the United States*. Many Native American names are included. For information on how to obtain this book search by the title or "Books by John Stemmons" at Amazon.com. This comes automatically with a paperback binding. It includes but is not limited to petitions regarding:

- "One of twelve men selected by the Cumberland people to govern the settlement, 1783; appointed by the Governor of North Carolina judge of the courts, Davidson County, 1783.
- Appointments about military and local officers, etc.
- Name on the "Treaty of Holston", 2 Jul 1791 between the President of the US and "Chiefs and Warriors of the Cherokee Nation of Indians."
- Memorial, 1 Aug 1791, to the President from the civil and military officers of Mero District explaining recent depredations of the Indians and seeking an "Act of Cession" from North Carolina.

95 pages $19.00

TN-02 TENNESSEE PETITIONERS, ETC. AND GRAINGER COUNTY TAX LISTS 1800 [1795-1804]© Compiled by John Stemmons, 2021. Also known as Territory South of Ohio River. This book was assembled from Grainger County Tax Lists 1800 and *Territorial Papers of the United States* and contains 182 names for the *Papers* and 247 names for the tax lists. From *Territorial Papers of the United States* the names mostly seem to be persons appointed to official or military positions or are members of the Knoxville Convention. Thus, they seem to be the more prominent persons, so, most of the less noteworthy individuals would not be listed. Still, the people listed clarify this early time before Tennessee became a state. The tax lists record the names of those who are taxable and are much more inclusive. They do include important details about the property they held. For information on how to obtain this book search by the title or "Books by John Stemmons" at Amazon.com. This comes automatically with a paperback binding. It includes but is not limited to petitions regarding:

- List, 21 Dec 1795, of members of Knoxville Convention.
- Appointments of military and local officers, etc.

49 pages $9.80

TN-03 TENNESSEE GRAINGER COUNTY TAX LISTS 1810 [1805-1814]© Compiled by John Stemmons, 2021. This book was assembled from Grainger County Tax Lists 1810 and contains 1242 names of those who are taxable. They do include important details about the property they held and may provide clues regarding relationship, etc. For information on how to obtain this book search by the title or "Books by John Stemmons" at Amazon.com. This comes automatically with a paperback binding.
146 pages $29.20

TN-04 TENNESSEE GRAINGER COUNTY TAX LISTS 1820 [1815-1824]© Compiled by John Stemmons, 2021. This book was assembled from Grainger County Tax Lists 1820 and contains 1161 names of those who are taxable. They do include important details about the property they held and may provide clues regarding relationship, etc. The lists for 1800-1820 furnish an excellent opportunity to track the population growth of the county. For information on how to obtain this book search by the title or "Books by John Stemmons" at Amazon.com. This comes automatically with a paperback binding.
131 pages $26.20

VA-01 VIRGINIA PERSONAL PROPERTY TAX LISTS, 1780 [1775-1784] (Accomack and Albemarle Counties)© Compiled by John Stemmons, 2021. This book was assembled from Accomack and Albemarle Counties Personal Property Tax Lists ca 1780 and contains

2553 names of those who are taxable. They do include important details about the property they held and may provide clues regarding relationship, etc. They even furnish the entry for, it is assumed, future president Thomas Jefferson! For information on how to obtain this book search by the title or "Books by John Stemmons" at Amazon.com. This comes automatically with a paperback binding.
252 pages $50.40

VA-02 VIRGINIA PERSONAL PROPERTY TAX LISTS, 1790 [1785-1794] (Accomack and Albemarle Counties)© Compiled by John Stemmons, 2021. This book was assembled from Accomack and Albemarle Counties Personal Property Tax Lists ca 1790 and contains 2679 names of those who are taxable, plus 3 from *Territorial Papers of the U.S.* They do include important details about the property they held and may provide clues regarding relationship, etc. They even furnish the entry for, it is assumed, future president Thomas Jefferson! Data on the age range of males is also included. For information on how to obtain this book search by the title or "Books by John Stemmons" at Amazon.com. This comes automatically with a paperback binding.
333 pages $66.60

VA-03 VIRGINIA PERSONAL PROPERTY TAX LISTS, ca 1800 [1795-1804] (Accomack and Albemarle Counties)© Compiled by John Stemmons, 2021. This book was assembled from Accomack and Albemarle Counties Personal Property Tax Lists ca 1800 and contains 3788 names of those who are taxable. They do include important details about the property they held and may provide clues regarding relationship, etc. They even furnish the entry for, it is assumed, future president Thomas Jefferson! Data on the age range of males is also included. With the lists for 1780-1800 one can track population growth in these countries. An individual showing up for the first time may indicate potential age. For information on how to obtain this book search by the title or "Books by John Stemmons" at Amazon.com. This comes automatically with a paperback binding.
436 pages $87.20

Population estimates were obtained from U.S. Bureau of the Census, *Historical Statistics of the United States, Colonial Times to 1957*, Washington, D.C., 1960, Library of Congress Card No. A 60-9150; and United States. Bureau of the Census, *A Century of Population Growth From the First Census of the United States to the Twelfth, 1790-1900* Washington: Government Printing Office, 1909. A household size of 5.7 persons was assumed.

Good morning.
We received the gift book of "Georgia Petitions 1785-1794". Fantastic book and a great tool in researching that time period. I like the format which is easy to read and puts in one place the petitions for research. I personally have searched many of the petitions and love this new tool. The introduction and the list of petitions gives much added information to understanding the petitions for the various individuals.
I look forward to ordering more books in July after our budget is in place. Thank you for contacting our library and making us aware of your fine publications. Have a great day.
Thanks,
Irene Godwin
Ellen Payne Odom Genealogy Library
204 5th St. S.E.
P.O. Box 2828
Moultrie, GA 31768

EXAMPLES OF THE KIND OF INFORMATION CONTAINED IN OUR BOOKS

Cicotte, J. Bte.,   Michigan Territory, District of Detroit, "Cote des Poux"
    Cicotte, J. Bte.,   45-Over? Male   **Color:**   White
    10-16   Male   **Color:**   White
    10-16   Male   **Color:**   White
    16-26   Male   **Color:**   White
    45-Over   Female   **Color:**   White
1810 Census of the District of Detroit
MS/Witherell (B. F. H.) Collection, LMS, Burton Historical Collection, Detroit Public Library, Folder 2
Cicotte, Jacques,   Michigan Territory
    Cicotte, Jacques,   Male
Petition, 26 Oct 1807, to Congress from inhabitants of Michigan Ter. seeking time to file claims to their land, claims on 1+ parcels be confirmed, farms on Detroit River be extended to 80 arpents, & occupancy later than 1 Jul 1796 be allowed [pp. 138-49].
Territorial Papers of the US - volume: 10 page: 146
Holeday, Jas,   Territory NW of Ohio River   Knox County, Vincennes
    Holeday, Jas,   Male
Address to Colonel Josiah Harmar by American inhabitants of Post Vincennes dated 4 Aug 1787
Territorial Papers of US - volume: 2 page: 65
Holliday, Heirs of James,   Territory NW of Ohio River   Knox County, Vincennes
    Holliday, Heirs of James,   Male
Petition, 7 Aug 1797, to Congress by inhabitants of Knox County, who migrated to Vincennes around 1786 and received land, but never obtained a deed.
Territorial Papers of US - volume: 2 page: 621
Lajoye, Pierre ,   Spanish North America, St. Louis
    Lajoye, Pierre,   Male
"Pierre Lajoye, formerly of Prairie du Rocher on the American side of the Mississippi".
Letter, 1790, by Governor St. Clair to Manuel Perez concerning an American boy in the possession of Pierre Lajoye [pages 237-238].
"Mr. Mayet has just complained to me that a Mr. La Joye, to whom he has entrusted an American boy, whom he took from the savages, to be returned to the parents of the latter, has not returned him, but is holding the boy as a slave and refuses to return the boy to them on the pretext of some debt. I am convinced that you will not find it proper that a free child should be held as a slave for the debts of another--and will order Mr. La Joye to return him to Mayet."

Letter, 26 May 1790, from St. Louis by Manuel Perez to Governor St. Clair concerning an American boy in the possession of Pierre Lajoye [pages 237-240]:

"MY DEAR SIR: In order to take cognizance of the subject of the claim in your favor of the 20th instant concerning the child who is today in the possession of Mr. Lajoye, I had the latter appear before me and from the questions which I put to him and the reasons which he advanced to me on this subject I have found in him only a disposition to render service to the Unhappy Father who lost him and who asks for him in a letter of which the said Mr. Lajoye is the bearer.

After studying this matter carefully, I find that the above-mentioned child claimed by Mr. Mayet can leave the possession of Mr. Lajoye only to go to that of the Father now living at Natches. I think also that it is just for the said Mr. Mayet to be reimbursed for what he actually gave the savages in order to get him out of their barbarous hands; . . .

When the young man arrived at Mr. Lajoye's house, he came and notified me of it at once and that he would write to the lower part of the Colony to learn in what district the Father of the said child lived. He learned later from the letter of which he is the bearer, that he resides at Natchez; accordingly he will send him down on the first opportunity."

Territorial Papers of the US - volume: 2 page: 237

Mayfield, Geddeon, Kentucky Barren County

Mayfield, Geddeon, Male

Acres of land: 200; Barren Co.; watercourse: Mill Creek; Entry: Geddeon Mayfield; Survey: same; Patent: 0; white males over 21: 0; white males 16-21: 0; blacks over 16: 0; total blacks: 0; horses: 0; stud horses: 0; retail stores: 0; tavern license: 0.

Barren County Tax Book, 1800, part 1 - page: 10 FAMILY HISTORY LIBRARY film 7865

LEGISLATIVE PETITIONS

Petitions to the governor, legislature, etc., were a particularly important way for individuals to communicate with their government regarding issues that were very essential to them. Their influence in making changes throughout our history has contributed to making our society what it is today. They are an important link in our legislative and judicial history. In these early petitions one can trace the growing desire for democracy. In fact, they are one of the most visible manifestations of democracy in practice. It is fascinating to view the changes in the reasons for submitting petitions over time (see the lists below.)

Because petitions represent the feelings of one or more individuals, they provide a window into the soul of the petitioners that illuminates the historical landscape. Most aspects of the human condition are addressed in some form by these important documents. The names listed with the petition can be used as a census of inhabitants for a particular locality. Often it is possible to determine useful information about individual persons from these records. They can help compensate for lost or destroyed county records. Petitions are original records that contain historical background about our culture and society.

Unfortunately, petitions are among the most inaccessible and underused records because there are so many, they are often difficult and time-consuming to read, and are usually housed only in the state archives or other repository in their un-microfilmed condition.

To help resolve this problem, we have abstracted the content of many petitions and indexed the names of the petitioners. A brief context of the petition is provided with each name. Generally, we have not included those petitions with fewer than 10-12 names.

GENEALOGY AND LOCAL HISTORY BOOKS IN PDF FORMAT ON A FLASH DRIVE

705 Local and Family History books for $75-or 11 cents a book!!! All 4 volumes of Savage's Genealogical Dictionary of New England would cost you about $0.44!*

You can have in your library/home more books of this type than most libraries have. They cover nearly all aspects of human experience including law, medicine, biography, history, etc., etc.

Concerns?

1. **Question:** I am uncomfortable in letting patrons use this small drive as it may become lost.

Answer: Simply download the contents of the drive onto your computer(s) and keep the drive in a safe place. We will replace it at no charge if it becomes lost.

2. **Question:** Some of our books, including those on microfilm, that are also on your flash drive are in poor condition because of patron use through the years, especially when copies are made. Copies made from microfilm are not always the best quality. How can you help us with these problems?

Answer: Once our books are on your computers, your originals can be kept in a secured area so that no more damage will occur because of hands-on use. The images on the computer can be easily printed, usually with better quality.

3. **Question:** We are only interested in items covering the locality our patrons live in.

Answer: Many of your patrons were born outside of your area and/or have ancestry from all over the United States, etc.

4. **Question:** Are these books under copyright restrictions?

Answer: They are in the public domain and so are not copyrightable.

Approximately how many pages do the 705 books add up to?
Total cost (from Stemmons Publishing) for hard copies: $7044 (not available now)
Approximated total pages of text on the flash drive: 221,307
Approximated total images on the flash drive: 58,272

A huge genealogical library of 705 books on your computer for only $75
A dealer's discount is available of $45 for 5 or more flash drives.
Imagine 705 books… 60,417 images… 230,642 pages on a small flash drive.

You may be able to find these books on Google, Ancestry, or FamilySearch. To make a hard copy from these sources may be expensive, especially if you were to copy all 705! I may be mistaken, but I'm not sure you can print just a single page from those services. You can with my books. You also have them immediately at your fingertips without needing to go to the effort to search these other services.
The downside to these books is that many are not indexed.
No problem: just check the index provided by these other sources before using our books.
"In 2016, popular genealogy blogger Dick Eastman surmised that perhaps ninety percent of the resources you may need to fill out your family tree are not yet available on the Internet." This statement was found on the Boston Public Library website. If that is true, some of the books on our flash drive may not be found on the Internet.

You may obtain a copy of the drive by sending check, money order, or cash to John Stemmons at 1078 Shields Lane, South Jordan, Utah, 801-254-2152 (Call between 9:00 a.m. and 5:00 p.m. Monday through Friday. If no one answers, please leave a message.), stemmonspublishing@gmail.com. We have been in this business since 1975! Check BBB if you need to.

The fee for shipping and handling is $10.00 unless you send a shipping container, deliverable to you, with sufficient postage to mail to you. Please allow 4-6 weeks for delivery.

The books on the drive are in the public domain and are not copyrighted. You may make as many copies of them as you would like. Please do not place the contents of the drive, in part or in full, on the Internet except for individual pages.

We do not do credit cards and PayPal. If you are unhappy with the drive, please return it for a refund of your money.

If you would like a list of questions and answers or a list of the books, please let us know.

*How are we able to do this? Simply by reducing each page so that 2-6 pages can be placed on a single 8½ by 11 sheet of paper and still be readable. With the computer, you can enlarge it as many times as needed.

Number of books by locality:
US-99, Regional-32, AL-1, CT-31, DE-1, GA-2, IL-1, IN-1, KY-1, ME-23, MD-15, MA-91, MI-1, MN-1, MO-2, NH-20, NJ-28, NY-81, NC-9, OH-9, PA-51, RI-6, SC-26, VT-2, VA-47, WV-1; Family History-62; CN-5; EN-39; IR-10; SCOT-7=705 books!